'Of all the ways you can kill yourself, using a bottle of tomato sauce is, I suspect, uncommon, says the narrator in this unusually frank account of a life of addiction. To which I might add: of all the ways to kill a person, pummelling him or her to death with knobkerries of dry humour is equally uncommon.

'Writing about addiction is risky business. The writer risks being preachy and self-righteous, or fucking boring and judgmental. In this no-holds-barred tale, Chilimigras achieves an unusual feat of sharing some intimate slices of a life dangerously lived, without being melodramatic or over the top. It's a controlled confession littered with landmines of dangerous humour, the kind that will get you kicked out of bed if you, like me, are one of those who do a lot of reading in it.

'But when you're finished laughing you can't help but sit back and think. Very hard.'

– FRED KHUMALO, AUTHOR OF DANCING THE DEATH DRILL

Things Even
González Can't Fix

Christy Chilimigras

First published by MFBooks Joburg, an imprint of
Jacana Media (Pty) Ltd, in 2018

10 Orange Street
Sunnyside
Auckland Park 2092
South Africa
+2711 628 3200
www.jacana.co.za

ISBN 978-1-928420-20-0

Cover design by Anastasya Eliseeva
Set in Sabon 11/15pt
Printed and bound by ABC Press, Cape Town
Job no. 003260

See a complete list of Jacana titles at www.jacana.co.za

Contents

For Nicole,
For everything

For Nic,
Who always told me to just fucking write

For Jenny,
With the tiny handwriting

CHAPTER 1

Bandy Legs and Black Bob

We are a family of addicts. Of overachievers. Of failures that we have given birth to and nursed and smothered. We are generous. Gullible. We wear middle partings and all sound the same when we cry. We are selfish, disillusioned passers-of-the-buck-constantly-hungry-Greeks. We are racists and homophobes. We are liberal to the point of screaming matches and then we dissolve into a smug, quiet confidence. We thrive on chaos. We avoid conflict – and conflict resolution. We eat and eat and eat. And we run. We run away. To Cape Town. To our rooms. To a studio apartment. We choose shit romantic partners. We have spastic colons and thinning hair. We feel inadequate. We are vain. We hold tight to the belief that we are meant to struggle. We have a sense of entitlement. We are liars.

We. A family. That smothers and cries and eats and shits on love.

***

I was born bald in 1993. A bald, fat, Greek second baby to a gorgeous Greek woman, whom I call Old Lass, and a Greek man known for his charm and bandy legs, My Father. Their firstborn, my sister – known here as Protector & Soul – was a fair, scrawny baby, who had arrived two years earlier, in 1991. Her body skinny in the way that makes babies 'beautiful', skinny in the way that defies 'cute'.

Old Lass met My Father when she was 23. Working in a small boutique at the time, she would armour herself in crisp white shirts boasting fine brooches and 'funky shorts and boots'. Her exquisite, round face was framed by a black bob. Her new nose, gifted to her by her parents for her twenty-first birthday, somewhat disguised her glaringly Greek roots.

Introduced to My Father by her brother, Old Lass recalls the distinct lack of – as she so eloquently puts it – the *gadoof*. That feeling that it was 'meant to be'. Rather, she saw My Father as the cultural plaster a young Greek woman puts over the wound of a lost Jewish love. She had adored Clive, his friends, the herring and kichel she'd dive into on Friday nights in his family home. She was patient with his parents, who seemed underwhelmed by her, as they were by everyone. She respected them, their culture and faith with a depth carved by her devotion to their son. However, when it came time to committing herself to their life, she thought of her own culture, her own traditions. Of Christmas. Of Greek Easters. Of dyeing boiled eggs red with her father the Thursday before Good Friday. Of tanned skin sizzling beneath a layer of olive oil under the Mykonos sun.

If she couldn't convert herself into the circle that a round hole required, she would find another – a tanned, guilt-laden Greek square peg – with whom she would fit. Over time, she allowed herself to be taken by My Father's charm. In the community to which my parents belonged, he was known as the life and soul of the party. For the Greek Zeibekiko dance, My Father would take the floor at gatherings, a pulsating wave of Greeks whirling around him. Whistling their whiskey-soaked breath in his direction from a knelt knee, plates would shatter around him and floors doused in liquor would be set alight. For this he was known. For this he was adored and revered, tears occasionally streaming from his calm eyes as he danced, so moved was he to dance to the notes of the bouzouki, amid the rosemary scent of roasted lamb. No one moved like him, and no one would forget him once he moved.

Only a breath into dating, on 30 June 1990, My Father and Old Lass were married. Protector & Soul arrived the next year, bundled into a gorgeous double-storey home in Sunninghill. The owner of a computer company (floppy discs were all the rage) – one of the first of its kind in Johannesburg – My Father spent his money on making this home just-so. An elaborate stairway led to finely furnished bedrooms. My mother, gifted a brand-new car tied in a pink bow as a Valentine's Day gift, wanted for nothing, and it wasn't long before she discovered that I was on the way. Old Lass had her life set out for her: a young, blonde, tantrum-throwing child at her side, and a bulging belly in which I was growing. My Father had his business, his friends – who all had their own businesses – and the cocaine that accompanied them on their daily comings and goings. 'The businessman's drug', all the better to get them up and keep them busy.

My Father's cocaine habit led him to a life spent chasing. It wasn't long before someone handed him a pipe. In later years, he would tell me that he didn't even know what crack was at that point. The pipe was just another rung on a rickety ladder to the sensational, heavenly sky to which cocaine beckoned him, an illusion that would eventually rob him of everything. Eventually the cells in his body belonged to another universe, the angels descending around him, comforting him, loving him, obsessing over him, fucking him. Soon he was no longer of this place, this place of Sunninghill homes and the pregnant belly of a wife with a round face and a perfect nose. He was living his new purpose, sweeping him higher-higher-higher than elaborate stairways or white powder trails had ever allowed him to go. There he was, My Father. And there he would remain, chasing that high, only to plummet downwards. Again and again for the rest of his life.

While I'll never know how My Father truly felt the first time he put a crack pipe to his lips (my dedication to the craft of writing falls short of lunging myself into the deep end of filthy rocks for the sake of aptly portraying a scene), he told me about his first crack high when I was about eight years old and he, his life now depleted, had moved back into his childhood home, where Old Lass was not. We sat on the veranda, the sun glistening beyond the old, warped windows, begging me to run outside. To run away. To be a child rather than learn about crack. Be a child. Be a child.

Instead, I was told that the angels do exist, that he saw them. I was told that a body can feel as though it is made of gold, made by God. I was told that that one moment was worth a lifelong chase, one moment to live for, die for, exist for, never again to be obtained. I was told that that day, that first high, was 'the best day of his life'.

'What is cocaine, Daddy?'

'What's crack?'

'Who gave it to you?'

'Why did they give it to you?'

'Did it really feel that good?'

The sun screamed. Be a child. Be a child. My heart ached. I couldn't wait to tell my friends what this thing called 'crack' was. My dad had seen the angels. My heart was racing.

Later I am told by Old Lass that on the day My Father first sucked on a crack pipe, he returned home. Late. I was in my sixth month in my mother's belly. My lungs were developing, bracing themselves for breath. My movements were becoming more powerful. Here the fuck I am, world. Place a hand on this round belly and await my arrival.

Old Lass, my lovely home, knew the minute My Father walked through that door that he had dipped his toe into the deepest end. She said she could see it in his eyes. They glistened furiously as he told her about the pipe he had just feasted on. She saw in his eyes his conviction. Saw that he was no longer there, with her. The veins in his eyes were now nothing more than a map to his next visit with the angels. As the months and years went by, Old Lass would look to these eyes of his for confirmation of his condition. 'All you need to do is look a person in the eye to know if they are high,' Old Lass would tell me when I was older, more grown up,

4

maybe 10 years old, medium-rare, not yet well done, 'They'll have a crazed look in their eye. I'd look your father in the eye. That was how I knew. Look people in the eye, Christy.'

I am born stargazing on a Sunday evening in September, and come home to a life that has descended into chaos. Old Lass, still trying to wrap her head around the fact that her jewellery is swiftly disappearing, trying to fathom the new friends My Father brings round for dinner, doesn't utter a word to her family about her husband's condition. One evening, she receives a call from a friend of My Father, known to everyone as Charlie Brown. She is instructed to pack a bag for herself and her two children as quickly as possible; he is on his way to fetch her. So my mom, my infant self and Protector & Soul are packed into Charlie Brown's car and are driven to the hotel at which My Father is waiting, hiding from the Nigerian dealers he has wronged. Once at the hotel, Old Lass phones her father, who up until this point has no idea of the turbulent life his daughter and granddaughters are being dragged through. Pappou, in turn, contacts his dear friend, Lieutenant Peach (you truly can't make this stuff up), who calls in whatever illegal favours are required of him to eradicate the problem that has led my family into hiding. Once resolved, Peach never speaks to my grandfather again. We return to our Sunninghill home the following day.

The following few months are awash with nappy changes, riddled with arguments over missing jewels, christening crosses, withering, withering, withered. When I am six months old, Old Lass is handed an incredibly large sum of money by My Father, with which she books flights for herself and her children, and takes to the sky to visit her mom in London for two weeks. There are photos from this trip of Protector & Soul and I lounging in a park with our grandmother whose tigerprint tracksuit speaks to the character of a woman who has been '54 years old' for as long as I can remember. Before long, the two-week trip comes to an end and Old Lass finds herself perched atop her suitcase at Johannesburg International Airport, shushing and consoling my sister and me as she waits for her husband to show up.

'I saw a man walking towards me. I didn't realise it was your father until he was right in front of me. Tiny, skinny. I still can't wrap my head around what those two weeks had been for him,' Old Lass tells me when I am 24 years old.

'You think that's why he gave you so much money, Mom? To get rid of you and us?' I ask her.

Old Lass pauses, takes it in. 'How stupid of me … That never occurred to me then. But, yes, I guess so. He wanted to get rid of us.'

I have been told – and will continue to be told for the rest of my life – that addiction is a disease. Like cancer, the truth of My Father eventually spreads through the extended family. Like cancer, the disease unites some and tears apart others. Unlike cancer, there is nothing subtle hiding beneath the surface; a sneaky sinister something that acts slowly, wearing you down from the inside out. The addiction, this disease, begins to present itself plainly in the form of tins of teething powder cut with cocaine. In the form of a mother who hides upstairs with her babies, wracking the map of her memory to figure out at what point she had turned right and her husband had turned left. It is a cheeky, brazen, sinister something that wears My Father down from the outside in. And there is nothing subtle about it.

The first Greek word I'll come to learn is 'Nona'. It means godmother. Mine is my mother's sister, and she is made of smooth edges. Her deep, curly black hair has a life of its own, but other than this she is a perfectly manicured mother to two boys. On a Saturday evening in my life's first summer, she hosts a dinner party. She and my Nono (my godfather) have invited a doctor husband, a social worker wife. As she busies herself in the kitchen, her landline rings. She knows immediately that something is wrong and that that something is My Father. When my Nona answers, she hears Old Lass breathless with fear on the other end of the line.

You need to come here now.

Please god, help me.

You need to come here now, it's Their Father.

My Nona screams – dinner party be damned – for her husband

to get to the Sunninghill house right away. She stays with her two young boys.

When my Nono pulls up at the house, he finds My Father clutching Protector & Soul to his side with one skinny arm and one manic hand, a gun in the other. He is threatening to shoot her. He is high and tiny and in this moment he has the capacity to be the force behind the biggest thing that will ever happen to our family. Old Lass is hysterical and is unable to get close enough him to grab my sister because every time she tries, he threatens to pull the trigger. Nono is calm.

'I'll give him this, in a crisis there is no one better to have around than your Nono,' my Nona tells me now, many years after their divorce.

Give me the child.

Give me the child.

You can't kill your baby.

Do whatever you need to do, but you can't kill this child.

Eventually, he talks My Father down. Once he's grabbed Protector & Soul, he tells Old Lass to fetch me from my crib. Once again, Old Lass and her two baby girls are packed into a car. Nono takes us home with him where the dinner party has died a premature death and mattresses have been set up on a bedroom floor.

At 9 am the next morning, the landline rings again. My Nona answers, already knowing who it is.

'Hi, Stasi,' My Father says. 'Do you by any chance know where my family is? I woke up this morning and there's no one at home.'

'The fucker didn't remember a thing,' my Nona tells me now.

My Father and mother last two years in the Sunninghill home before their livelihood is set alight and devoured, snatched away. Old Lass, never fully or even remotely accepted by My Father's family (the poor woman wasn't 'Greek' enough for them), would stand guard at his door while he lay down, low down, crashing in his office. Face down in his life that was falling to pieces.

One day she finds the strength to call my Nono.

'I need your help.'

A shit storm swiftly descends over my parents. My Father is sent to Riverfield Lodge, a rehabilitation centre where Old Lass would bring Protector & Soul to visit him – a decision she would later deeply regret. My infant state protects me from such visits. But before he has been there long enough to let the lodge and its teachings sink in, he absconds. He returns to his children, to a wife who is adamant to make her marriage work. No longer able to afford the two-storey Sunninghill dream house, our family of four bounce between new houses, never settling long enough to grow roots.

CHAPTER 2

Attempted Death by Condiment

Of all the ways you can kill yourself, using a bottle of tomato sauce is, I suspect, uncommon. One day, when my mother returns from grocery shopping to the tiny townhouse into which she has poured herself after having to leave behind her palace, all so white, so clean – everything that her life was not – she must have thought to herself, 'Here lie grocery bags, the makings of a meal the crack addict will not arrive home to eat.'

But he does. There he is among the white. There he exists in the white, the white of his rocks, the white of his disgusting nostrils.

The white of my mother's pillows.

The floors.

The couches.

All white.

And on his descent from his heavenly hell, he lunges for a glass bottle of tomato sauce, ripping it from the plastic bag that has just been set on the floor.

Not white.

Red.

All gold.

And he promptly proceeds to smash the glass to his head.
Red.
Red.
Red.
Sweet.
Salty.
Iron.
Fucked pillows.
Fucked floors.
Fucked couches.
'Here lies Mr Chilimigras. Attempted death by condiment.'

My Father rushes, dripping blood and tomato sauce, through the small townhouse to the bathroom and, on his way, he grabs his gun. He stands in the white shower and touches the muzzle of the gun to his temple.

Old Lass watches, calmly. She knows it is her turn to talk him down now. And so she does.

I am a teenager when I hear this story for the first time. I have begun digging through my mother's soil to recover my own roots.

'I suppose it's the polite thing to do, to do it in a shower, if you're going to shoot yourself in the head,' she tells me when I have successfully nagged her into telling me the full story. 'Although I was irritated that he hadn't taken the tomato sauce bottle into the shower with him in the first place.'

Old Lass and I laugh. The world is a Greek stage, and we are comedians in our pain.

'I should have let him shoot himself in the head that day.' The world is a Greek stage, and I nod in agreement.

Before Old Lass does finally leave him, My Father is always leaving. Either of his own volition or because Old Lass insists upon it. And then he returns. My parents continue to live in their elastic world: they break, go their own way. They return. They break. They return. When this process finally becomes too tiresome for Old Lass, she leaves My Father once and for all, a two-year-old and four-year-old hanging on to her linen shirt hems and tanned calf muscles.

In a panic I suspect is altogether too familiar for single mothers, Old Lass knows she has to start making money asap. With this in mind, she throws herself into a gloriously beautiful store called the Splodge Shop. Catering to the rich and manicured mothers of Johannesburg, she creates children's furniture and other home goods that are so gorgeous and unique they more than justify their steep price.

Protector & Soul and I spend hours with her in her shop. We trace our fingers along fabric swatches and lounge on the small armchairs that will soon be sent off to children far fancier than we are. With this shop, Old Lass becomes our hero.

I devote a child's eternity to sniffing the handmade flower-shaped soaps. Greedily inhaling the red ones – they smell the best – a smooth, long wooden stick piercing their lovely flower bottoms. I remember with absolute clarity, and heartbreak, one particular day spent sniffing. Like spritzing yourself with your most beloved perfume only to become immune to your own, expensive scent, so the sodomised flower soaps would lose their scent as I sniff them. Of course, at this age I have not yet worn perfume, not yet had the opportunity to learn the lesson of fleeting scent that has never left in the first place. The usual routine consists of saving, of course, the best red for last. Three sniffs of the green flower soap, divine and then scentless. Four sniffs of the orange flower soap, satisfying and then a bore. Two sniffs of the blue, four of the yellow, and then on to the last, the red, the favourite. As my nostrils collapse in on themselves, furiously inhaling, it occurs to me that each and every time I smell one of my mother's flower soaps dry, I am stealing the quality that prompts people to purchase them. *Who will buy soaps that have had the smell smelled out of them? I've damaged an entire batch of soap. I've robbed it of its soapy essence, stolen from it its purpose. Dear God, I've put my mom out of business.* From that day on, I never sniff those soaps again, and am never consoled into doing so because I am too nervous to tell Old Lass what I've done. Spiral, spiral, spiral. I mourn now for those childlike spirals. I'd give anything to smell the smell out of something beautiful again.

CHAPTER 3

Channelling Elton

After bouncing from house to home during my parents' separation, off we flit, the three Chilimigras girls, and settle in a two-bedroom flat in Wendywood. This is the first home I clearly remember living in. What turns our minds into sponges between the ages of four and five, I don't quite know, but a sponge my mind was. As I sit writing now, I'm able to recall every corner, every Christmas beetle of that home.

My Pappou lives in a flat above us, just to the left. I have always thought he is a rather beautiful man. He has a round face that my mother and I have both inherited, more becoming on him than I believe it to be on either of us. He has dark marks on his face that grow year by year, and a crown of thinning grey hair that remains unaltered in my eyes until the day he dies. He wears thick glasses and carries his jersey in a plastic shopping bag, and if you stare at him for long enough he looks almost Asian.

Days spent playing in our small, sloped garden beneath his flat are forever accompanied by the aromas of his homemade chilli sauce. When my sister and I make the adventure up the black stairwell to his flat, the smells would greet us from behind even a closed door. The scent of peppercorn clung to his knitted waistcoat, TCP antiseptic lingering on his breath as he whispers that that is his secret to good health. His tiny balcony is home to the chillies he has birthed from seed gathered from Mozambique and Cyprus. Grow to harvest to keep to feed. His chilli sauce, an unending opportunity to devour sentimentality. I feel saddened now as an adult that I didn't spend more time in his home as a child. That I didn't pore over his collection of black-and-white photos and take him up on his offers of spaghetti bolognaise. But his bolognaise always contained entirely intact and softened peppercorns, which I couldn't wrap my young, whimsical head around. Besides, there was an entire flat packed with my sticker books, Barbies and pets downstairs begging for my attention. With our childhood beckoning, Protector & Soul and I would flit away from his flat as quickly as we had arrived there.

When he would occasionally make the great trek downstairs to visit his daughter and granddaughters, he would sit at the table and pick at the tuna salad or the leftover pizza, or whatever it was my mom has set in front of him. I would always greet him with 'Hello, Pappouli,' and he in turn would say, 'Hello, my girl.' We'd hug and his long palm would pat my back to the rhythm of his greeting. Hello. My. Girl. This man had no idea how strong he was and I'd always walk away from these hugs smiling at a man who believed he had little life left in him, but could potentially still pound the life out of another.

My Pappou could tell stories. Long stories that were crafted with care and patience, with such intricate detailing that they could have been born from experiences of just yesterday. He'd tell stories that the family had heard countless times, that provoked sighs and slight smiles. Most of his tales would begin with 'Thirty years ago' and his pronunciation of the word 'thirty' was always one of my favourite things. The *i* of the 'thirty' would escape his lips in a high note, in a singsong manner that was drawn out and raised, and completely charming only because of the old mouth it came from. At an oval glass table that would go on to provide the frame for many a blanket fort in the years to come, the three generations would sit and eat and talk and sigh before he'd disappear once again up the dark stairwell, leaving his three girls rubbing his kind words, greetings and goodbyes, from our still-ringing backs.

In this, our new two-bedroomed home, Protector & Soul and I, along with our two best friends Brandon and Savannah, would put on Backstreet Boys concerts for our mothers. Five rand got you in. The four of us, a merry and mischievous gang dubbed 'The Dragons' would steal matches and set alight dry twigs under the washing line. We'd spend our hard-earned savings on BB guns from the flea market. We'd run through the black halls of the flats, at war with each other, at war with the world. It is here, in this home, that we'd convince Brandon that our Backstreet Boys concerts, while fabulous, were becoming tiresome and it was time we incorporated the Spice Girls into our repertoire. In this home, I would sit alone on the carpeted lounge floor, a single lit candle resting in front of my crossed legs, and screech along to Elton John's 'Candle in the Wind'. Then, at the end of the song, dramatically exhaling, blasting the flame into oblivion, before lighting it again and lambasting the neighbours' ears once more. In this home, the poet, the romantic, the Dragon and the child in me thrive. I fall asleep every night praying to wake up to snow … in the middle of a South African summer. In this home, I name my first pets, two goldfish, Romeo and Juliet – only to wake a few weeks later to find them both floating, dead, in the bowl. *Oh, the poetry of it all! For my two fish, Romeo and Juliet, to have pegged together, on the very same day!* In this home I learn how to exhale, to play, and never treat my pets again as though they are Greek, thus avoiding over-feeding them to an untimely death.

At this point, while I am living my best life, My Father moves back to his childhood home with his mother, my YiaYia. Located in Rosebank, the low walls of this home barely conceal the stereotypes that keep the *My Big Fat Greek Wedding* franchise going. Old furniture preserved in mint condition with the help of plastic covers adorns the lounge and the dining room and the other dining room (one to use, one only to look at). Old biscuit tins filled with useful and useless things can be found in every room. Here, My Father and my YiaYia speak to each other in Greek bursts, and while I never understand a word of it, I know their conversations aren't kind. My Father, still harbouring resentments from his early childhood, had proceeded to pack every issue he'd ever had with his mother neatly onto a shelf in his mind. Able to pick from the spines of his memory with feeling, eyes closed, he'd regale Protector & Soul and me with elaborate tales of all the ways in which she had failed him throughout his life. He would tell us, annunciating each heartbroken and heartbreaking syllable, how she'd never loved him as much as she did his sister, who was given a piano and a guitar and a car and he hadn't. She hadn't devoted as much of her attention or affection to him as she had with everyone else. She didn't love my sister and I as much as she loved our cousins, who were born to the favoured sibling. He wasn't good enough, and we weren't good enough. 'Look at how she brings your cousin chopped cucumber and tomato while he watches TV,' he'd remind us as he swung his arm in the direction of my younger, blonde cousin with his big, lovely head staring contentedly at the television screen. 'She doesn't do that for you. Oh, and, Christy, even though you're only six, she's told the family back in Greece that you're a poutana.'

'What's a "poutana", Daddy?'

'It means whore. Your grandmother tells everyone you're a whore.'

My YiaYia, always clad in the same dresses, the pale pinks and greens of thin cotton lined with white frills that Johannesburg housewives buy for their domestic workers, would shuffle from room to room, her loose brown sandals exposing the chunky, plum veins resisting compression beneath her nude tights. Despite her legs betraying her, she is known for her flawless complexion. The skin on her face refuses to warp even while her sunken cheeks invite it to turn to waves. Framing her youthful face is her pale brown hair that dances with the grey but never lets it take the lead.

Having moved to South Africa at the age of 17 to start a new life for herself with my Pappou Number Two, she slowly somewhat mastered the English language. But even after a near-lifetime here, words spoken in anything other than her native language fall heavily from her lips like rocks she's had to force out with a marshmallow tongue. Watching her through my young eyes in the mornings when I awoke in her home, I'd feel my frustration rise as she'd exhume a slice of white bread from within its packet before sliding it into an old, silver toaster. Once it abruptly popped up, only a few shades lighter than her houseboy, Paul, she'd carefully butter it. She'd slice it down the middle into two, oozing rectangles, and then with fluid movements, retrieve tin foil from the pantry, carefully wrap the toast, and lay it in a kitchen drawer next to where the cutlery slept. There the toast would sit untouched for two days, before she'd give in, tear it up, and toss it wildly into the air over the lawn, any number of birds waiting to be fattened up below. Having known what is was to be starving during her youth in Greece, she was adamant to always have food in her home, in her drawers, and, begrudgingly, finally in her neighbourhood pigeons. It didn't matter how long she'd been in this country, she simply wasn't of this country. Leaning in to me one day when I arrived at her front door with a childhood friend who'd come for a visit, she screamed in a whisper, 'Chrysanthy, do you know your friend is a *mavro?*'

Me, responding in an actual whisper, 'Yes, YiaYia, I know she's black.'

In another of my earliest memories, I am in the back seat of My Father's gold Toyota Corolla while my big sister, who at this point in her life is referred to as 'Tiger' by My Father, sits in the front seat with her tomboy-scabbed knees leaning dramatically to the left, away from the driver's seat, distorting herself to the point that she looks ready to break. We are reversing out of the driveway. He has his arm slung over my sister's seat to anchor his twisted body as he looks back, and says to me, 'Mouse, I don't care who you bring home. As long as he's white. And if he's Greek, that's a bonus.'

I like to think that even then, at the age of seven or eight, I was certain of at least two things:

1. Whatever a mouse lacked, a tiger made up for.
2. My Father was absolutely full of shit.

I don't remember when first we started spending every second weekend at My Father's house. It was always just our condition. The way it was.

In playschool, I remember how every second Friday morning saw a shell of a Christy. Slinking into the classroom, I'd haul my black weekend bag along with me. The teacher would pop it, effortlessly, onto the top of a shelf where it would wait until My Father picked us up at the end of the day. There on the shelf it would watch and weigh on my mind. Heavy and horrendous and existing. The only solace during my childhood Fridays in playschool came in the form of bread. Having sneakily befriended every young Jew I'd set my eyes on, I'd wait, eagerly and greedily outside of the Jewish Studies classroom to collect their challah on their way out. Revelling in each bite of the sweet bread and thanking my lucky stars that they were saving their appetites for the tastier loaves their mothers would be serving that evening during Shabbat.

Meanwhile, the struggle back home for Old Lass, trapped in the two-bedroom flat, a newly single mother, was to find an escape. Let your children go. Start smoking pot more regularly. Wait for them to come back. Let your children go. Attend a rave and drop some E with your best friend. Wait for your children to come home. Let your children go. Experience the recklessness you never allowed yourself to have in your twenties. Wait for your children to come home. Get stoned.

I still dream of that every-second-weekend house, the house My Father until today continues to share with his mother. Brown bricks. A glass front door, warped, all the better to see silhouettes approaching. Over the years, I have avoided that house by all means necessary. When excuses evaded me, in I'd walk and greet my demons before melting to my knees. As a child, I never knew how to walk through the carpeted halls of this place. I would run. There goes the hairy Greek girl – see how she gallops. With astonishing clarity and considerable heartbreak, I remember racing through the dark passages of my YiaYia's house, tears in my eyes, tearing from one room to the next, trying to outrun something I couldn't see but could feel breathing down my neck.

When Protector & Soul wasn't near me – God forbid she had left me in our shared bedroom alone – I would stand at the doorway. Minutes and lifetimes passed as I'd work up the courage. To outrun nothing and everything. To flee invisible demons and into the arms of tangible ones. To seek out my sister, to play Lego, to drink sweet tea. I always felt lonesome in this. Lonesome and ridiculous and furious with my sister for bravely walking without me. Years later, I asked Protector & Soul if she remembered how I would run through that house, envious that she'd been a 'normal' child, one who was able to walk. I asked if she knew why I did this.

'I don't remember exactly. I used to force myself to walk through it, though. If I ran, I felt like I was admitting defeat.'

CHAPTER 4

Scoring with my Father

I suppose My Father, in his drug-induced insanity, always believed he was doing the best he could for us. On second weekends, in the early hours of the morning when he would put us, ripped from sleep and dreams, into the back seat of his car for a crack excursion to Hillbrow, we would ask him to leave us at home. Our YiaYia was, after all, right there, asleep in her bed.

He would always say no. That we weren't safe with our grandmother, that we were safest with him. In the way that children absorb words as pearls and declarations as gold, we'd be both petrified and relieved to visit street corners at 3 am.

Men would casually approach My Father's car, expecting him. Expecting us. I giggle sickly now thinking of those shadowed dealers who must have revelled in the idiocy of this drug-addled white man. Motivated so by crack that he'd bring his young children along for the ride. We were badges of his stupidity. Badges of desperation. Perhaps we were armour. *Please, Mr Drug Dealer, be kinder to me. Give me credit. Don't you see my children pretending to sleep in the back seat of my car?*

When these Hillbrow visits first began, My Father would take us during the day. Daylight hours. Explorers of the city. Look left, look right, tales of what Hillbrow used to be. The clubs, the coffee shops, a time before the Nigerians arrived. With tourist eyes, we'd drink it all in before distorting our faces into grotesque masks and sticking out our tongues, chins raised, at Ponte Tower. 'All the baddies in Johannesburg live in Ponte Tower,' My Father tells us. 'You have to pull faces at them to show them you're not scared of them.' But the daylight visits ended, My Father sinking gloriously into the anonymity and darkness of the night.

Reversing out the driveway, leaving the cruel YiaYia at home at 3 am, I'd think of her failures, her shortfalls so delicately illustrated, painted with care, by My Father. And we'd head out to town. You know … because it was *safer*.

Away from the clutches of the villainous grandmother, stinking of mothballs, storing chocolates in her hoarder's paradise to give us for our birthdays. I remember swearing, as a child, that My Father's assertion that his mother was cruel must have been true. After all, she seemed to buy chocolates in 1998 to give to us in 2004. In 2004, she'd stock up for 2009 celebrations. What kind of sicko insists on gifting expired chocolate? The white age that creeps up the side of a once-perfect Ferrero Rocher would drive me into a silent rage. I would stare at the locked cupboards in that house, and fresh confectionaries would yell back at me. 'Eat me while I'm fresh – the old bat has taken us hostage. We've seen what's headed your way this Christmas, Mouse. And it ain't fucking pretty.' I never did dare find the keys and release those deliciously fresh captives. I was too busy running through the halls to be mischievous, sweet dreams yelling at me as I flew past.

Leaving Hillbrow each time, my dad would plan his exit strategy around one specific stretch of road. This strip of tar, abruptly dipping and then gently rising a few metres later, would send the car into a state of suspension if driven fast enough. There we would sit, Tiger in the front, Mouse in the back. Our organs free floated, our hearts spilled from our asses and our mouths in the same instant, our toes hovering above car mats. Screeches of delight accompanying us on the way down. We'd beg him to turn around and do it again. Sometimes he would. Sometimes he wouldn't. That hill became 'Christy's Hill'. From the beginning, when he and his crazed, contour-lined eyes would approach our beds, when his bony knees would kneel next to our little heads to wake us up – Tiger first, then Mouse, still half crusted in dream – we'd tell him we just wanted to sleep. And he would say, 'We're going to Christy's Hill, don't you want to fly?'

In those early years, as with every child, my parents held our lives in their hands. Old Lass, our comfort, working her fingers to the bone. Sandpaper caressing furniture. Palms floating recreational drugs to her lips every other weekend. Fingers stirring the bechamel that covered and crisped our pastitio, fingers curling duvet covers under our necks as she'd tuck us in. Fingers combing back our hair and buttoning our shirts. My Father, palms held out of car windows, hands clasped around a crack pipe, exposed our sanity and childhood to the chill of night air and reality and nightmare. My Father's limbs limp, as he'd die in his sleep for two days at a time when his upturned palms would fail him. His thumb grating away at his index finger, fidgeting. Fidget. Fidget. Wearing down what little sanity we had left. His hands locking his bedroom door every night when he sidled off to bed. My little hands. Tiny fists, knocking. Tentatively. My empty belly wanting toast. *Please wake up. Please stop sweating everywhere. Please stop dying for two days at a time – and feed us. Please stop lying, sloppily, wetly, on your back on a bed on the orange blanket that is absorbing your smell. Please wake up and be a dad. Use your fingers to make us a meal, use your hands to hold books to read us bedtime stories. Take your palms as far away from our bodies as you can. Wake up and feed us. Go away and die.*

Parents are curious things. They possess everything. The lessons we're forced to learn. The stories we're forced to listen to. The hands that pull away the fingers we've shoved into our ears. *I won't listen – you can't make me.* But they do. They make us. The hands to prise away the young, sticky palms we bury our eyes in.

I won't look – you can't make me. But they do. They make us. Whether they, or we, like it or not, they make us see and hear everything. Young minds and minds' eyes like sieves, like sponges. Young hearts and thumping cells like cemeteries. All things buried.

I must have been six or seven the first time I decide it's time I bath myself at My Father's house. Protector & Soul and I discuss it at length. She helping me build up the courage it would take for me to tell him that, like my sister, I was old enough to do it myself.

We cover all the angles. What I should say if he says this or points out that. Conversations, meetings like this between me and my sister, are not uncommon. We often sit together and discuss our feelings, attempt to piece ourselves back together. Later in life, this hands-on and unrelenting approach to communication I'd honed as a child drives my boyfriends insane. To them, it seems I exist only to harp on. Never letting go, never moving on. I try to explain that my intensive style of communication isn't intended to bleed them and our conversations dry. It is my goddamn lifeline. Spoken words like pegs in a tent, keeping me in place, keeping me anchored and of this world.

My Father's response, as we'd predicted, is one of panicked fury. 'You think you're fucking old enough to bath yourself?' he barks. 'You'd better do a good job because I'll be checking after.'

Minutes later my little body sits in the bathtub in that Rosebank house. My knees, my toes, my earlobes, all feel proud. I've fucking done it. I've eliminated the bathtime discomfort that has been settling into my bones like clockwork at 6 pm on the evenings I have been at My Father's house. I soap and rinse myself, careful to never use the bar of My Father's Clinique face soap he swears makes him look years younger than he is. 'Always dab your face dry, never wipe,' he'd say.

I soap and rinse. Soap and rinse. Great attention is paid to my belly button, always My Father's go-to location for rigorous scrubbing. I climb out the bath, body dripping onto the bathmat resting on the carpeted floor. The bathmat that always stinks of damp. Always. I dry myself. Beaming. Proud.

He walks in.

'You dry?'

'Yes, I'm dry.'

His bulging eyes crazy, his lips pursed, 'Let me check then.'

He runs his hands over my ankles. Up my calves. Up my thighs. In between my bum cheeks. The top of his hand grazes my source.

'You're not dry. You can't do this on your own. I told you. Wait here.'

He returns with a belt. He folds it over itself. He pulls and snaps it.

I barely remember anything after this other than sobbing. Being told to shut up or I'd be given something to cry about. I don't think he hit me with the belt then, but perhaps this is because everything is black. The snapping leather is a threat. A roaring warning. A reminder that I belong to him.

I remember my sister, the Tiger, telling me how brave I have been, how well I'd cleaned myself, and that we'd try again another time.

CHAPTER 5

Fuck the Birds and the Bees

It is on the same veranda, the one where my head would later swirl in My Father's crack pipe dreams, floating me up-up-up and away from my innocence, that I first learnt about the birds and the bees. In that one moment, I feel I should be grateful that where there is usually 'pee-pee', there was now 'penis'. That where parents forever ruin the deliciousness and carelessness of an edible 'cookie', there was 'vagina'. But having been on the receiving end of the PENIS-VAGINA conversation with My Father, I believe I would have preferred being put off cookies for the rest of my life. Perhaps there is a reason parents are reduced to nervous schoolchildren, their vocabulary abandoning them on the way down when it comes to conversations about S.E.X.

Protector & Soul and I sit opposite My Father on the veranda. He on a metal-legged chair with a turquoise vinyl finish, its seat hard and cracking under the weight of so many years and so many asses. My sister and I on a sunken couch that tries to swallow us whole into its brownness. Caged budgies chirp, balancing on ill-placed metal safes that serve as storage units, containing still more biscuit tins. I am six years old. My bony knees are scabbed, jungle gyms having bested me at break time. Tiger's knees are also scabbed, although hers more proudly so as she squared up to a fight in the Grade 3 playground. And so during the next half-hour, our defeated and defiant kneecaps become a view as demanding of our attention as Table Mountain.

'The man takes his penis, which has gotten really hard, and puts it into a vagina.'

The edges of our biltong scabs rise to meet our horror.

'Then he thrusts and thrusts and it should feel really good.'

Doesn't Brandon have a friend who eats his scabs?

Huh, that's so gross.

'Don't look so scared, Mouse. People love having sex.'

The sun screaming. Be a child. Be a child.

My insides screaming the same.

This must be what all parents tell their children. I wonder if the girls at school know about this feel-good thing: S.E.X.

Maybe a day or a week later, during a visit to the pharmacy with My Father, I notice the flavoured condoms hanging from metal rods on a display case.

'Daddy, why are these condoms flavoured?'

Not, 'What are condoms?' No, rather, 'Why are they flavoured?'

'They're flavoured because of this thing called a blow job. When a man puts his penis in a woman's mouth, that's a blow job. They're flavoured so that the blow job tastes nice so women don't complain about giving them.'

That's so considerate, to make this thing called a blow job taste nice.

In Grade 1, the teachers and I are not the greatest of friends. I am an odd child. A nervous child. A lively and then abruptly deathly child. In preschool I develop a habit I carry through with me to primary school, which makes it impossible for me to blend in to the decorated walls. I suck on my top lip. With conviction. Suck and suck until it bruises. A brown, purple throbbing moustache beneath my actual little sprouting moustache. Suck and suck and suck until my bruise is dry and cracking, up high enough to almost tickle my nose. I cry and cry and cry if I happen to misplace my lip ice. Once located, I draw the tubed Vaseline thickly onto my face. Bottom lip. Thin top lip. Bruise, bruise, bruise, back and forth I cake my cracking brown, sucked-dry, bruised lip with a sticky sheen. See how it glimmers, how it glows. The teachers beg me to stop. I go home and Old Lass begs me to stop. But I suck and suck and suck and then look in the mirror and cry at the bruised child looking back at me.

Apart from the warzone that's my under-nose, I carry other stubborn tendencies with me through the school hallways. Crayons: check. Books: check. Insistence on wearing my white school socks inside out: check.

My Grade 1 teacher screams at me to put them on correctly. Her otherwise fair face glowing irritably and pinkly from under a shaggy blonde bob. She looks at my act of defiance as an opportunity to make an example out of me. *Sit on the cold floor outside of the classroom and don't come in until you've fixed your socks.*

One day after Old Lass is made aware of her insubordinate child's refusal to be normal down to her very toes, my mother asks me why I won't just wear my socks the right side out. 'It feels like there are stones in my shoes when I wear my socks the normal way,' I tell her.

'What do you mean stones in your shoes? There are no stones in your shoes – and certainly not because of how you wear your socks.'

I pull off my school shoe, sock seams glaring at us, and touch my finger down on the sides of the stitching where toes are kept. I show my mother how the little worm seams grate my baby toes if worn as they should be. Old Lass, my mom, understands me. She tells me to ignore the teachers and wear my socks however I want to. She'll explain my discomfort to them.

At the end of Grade 1, the teachers decide that, going into the next year, I'll be best suited to the remedial class. Known as the 'Pilot Class', twelve children are crammed into a small, makeshift classroom hidden at the back of the school library. I adore this place. It has a low ceiling and a round bay window that looks out over a dark path lined with trees, preventing light from flooding our remedial existence. It feels like the safest space in the world, vowels drawn beautifully in chalk along the walls, over and over again by our new teacher, Mrs Carty. When I think of her now, standing in that classroom, she is ancient. I don't know if this is true, or whether my youth propped a fresh, 60-year-old woman onto the last legs of her life, but to me, she was ancient. Ancient and kind and scary and smoky. Each morning as we Pilot Class kids arrive into the belly of the library, Mrs Carty checks our lunchboxes. Anything with MSG or sugar is thrown out. I suspect I am the only child in the class who isn't on medication for some sort of attention deficit disorder, and so we are prohibited from artificial energy for fear that we'll vibrate through the roof, before shooting down again and suffering through the same school year multiple times in an effort to reach the same level as the 'normal' kids. Once our chips and smuggled biscuits are thrown out, while the hundred-or-so other Grade 2s begin the first lesson of the day, myself, a girl I'll call Shirley and the ten boys who make up the Pilot Class follow Mrs Carty to the main sports field, each child clutching their own activity toy of choice. The boys usually with a soccer ball each. Me armed with a skipping rope. Mrs Carty takes a seat at the bottom of the concrete grandstands, leaves swaying above her, while she lights a long cigarette. Inhaling deeply, she exhales into a whistle and off we go. The twelve most special and fucked-up kids running around the field chasing a ball or hopping over a rope, a supreme attempt at ridding us of any extra energy before commencing with our lessons on the A-E-I-O-Us.

I'm pretty sure it's during this two-year remedial period of my life that the fighter in me is established. In Grade 3, the Pilot Class, which is still made up of me, Shirley, and the ten boys, grows a fraction bigger with the arrival of a few devastated children who are dropped from the mass of regular students into our ranks. As the class grows, so our library refuge can no longer contain us, Mrs Carty, and the bins overflowing with crunchy contraband. We are moved into a god-awful classroom on a generic corridor, lined with more boring classrooms, all bursting with the nasty children who yell, 'You're going to fail' at us as we walk past them on our way to the tuck shop.

I suppose Shirley and I, being the only two girls in a world full of boys, could have bonded. But the bullying we suffer at the hands of the mainstream kids has soured us. In the afternoons we go home and sob in the arms of our parents about how mean the 'other' children are to us because we are 'special', and the next morning we arrive back at school and unleash all of our childish nastiness on Shirley. At such a young age, her acne-riddled face welts and blisters for weeks at a time, whiteheads littering her lovely, dark face as her braids, decorated with colourful beads, work overtime to draw the attention of others up-up-and-away from her face. And so I chant along with the boys, 'Shirley the pizza face with toppings on top,' while secretly pulling strands of hair from my ponytail over my bruised top lip.

Some of these boys and their skinny ankles are still deeply etched into my mind. There was Calvin-Sexy-Legs, whose big sister had died. I remember being moved that he and his family would still visit her favourite restaurant every year on her birthday. I giggle and choke now on the guilt at having sexualised a seven-year-old boy by referring to him as 'sexy legs'. There was David T. A tiny boy whose white skin would boil into red patches on summer days, causing a mottled appearance that would melt away and then angrily rise again after a fingertip would press down on it, before turning blue at the arrival of winter. There was Shane, who had secured the role of Peter Rabbit in the end-of-year play we were putting on (I wailed, Old Lass holding me, over the injustice that the mainstream kids had been allocated *Cinderella* for their own play while we were stuck with fucking *Peter Rabbit*). Shane had landed the lead role on a Friday morning, and I'd spent the rest of the day fuming – with myself mostly, for not having been brave enough to audition in the first place. By the time the final bell rung and little chairs were lifted onto little desks, I felt a fiery certainty that if I didn't act now, I'd forever regret it. As Mrs Carty began to bid us weirdoes goodbye, I shot up my hand and bellowed, 'Mrs Carty, I would like to audition for the role of Peter Rabbit.' Shane was peeved, man. He was especially peeved when Mrs Carty's mouth twitched into a knowing smile before telling me to go right ahead.

Right there next to my desk, with the seat of my chair level with my nervous head, I stood as tall as I could, breaking my back with a pride and posture it had never before experienced, plastering the most surprised expression I could muster onto my face, before flinging my skinny arm around to point at my ass, and saying, 'What's that? Whatever is it for?' Indeed, Peter Rabbit had just discovered his tail for the first time.

Mrs Carty clapped her hands together, just once, declaring, 'And Christy will play the role of Peter Rabbit.'

If you're feeling sorry for Shane, don't. He went on to spy and see me naked on a Grade 7 tour through a crack in the curtains, so … fuck Shane.

And then there was Lualan. That little asshole and I were the frontrunners in the comprehension activities that dear, cloudy Mrs Carty would have us do every day. The comprehensions were divided into categories based on difficulty, each category colour coded. Purple to some might represent 'sexual frustration', but to me, when I see purple, specifically dark purple, all I see is victory at having beaten Lualan to the finish line.

My elation was sorely short-lived, however, when December arrived and news broke that my days in the Pilot Class were coming to an end. Most of us, myself and Shirley included, had passed the year and were now allowed to fraternise with the enemy in the mainstream classes going into the next year, while others, namely Lualan, were held back to repeat Grade 3. Instead of being disappointed that my comprehension companion would no longer be around to challenge me, I quickly felt my dark purple pride dissipate. *Who cares if I beat Lualan at comprehensions if he's so stupid they held him back a year?*

CHAPTER 6

Mustard, Mustard and Heineken

Around this time, Old Lass meets the man that will become Second Husband. He's a tall, lanky antiques dealer whose body possesses not one Mediterranean bone. Protector & Soul and I immediately dislike him. We aren't used to such pale skin. We aren't used to men who actually do things, like go fishing, and who drag us along to do so. We aren't used to men who don't smoke crack and who instead drink beer, greedily, so that it dribbles from their lips. We aren't used to men who braai. We aren't used to having a loud, fishing, beer-drinking man in our house telling us what to do. And we definitely aren't used to having to share our mother. In our young and expert opinions, Second Husband wears far too much cologne, is far too literal in the colour coding of his outfits (sometimes arriving head to toe in coordinating shades of brown and mustard) and is simply not right for Old Lass. But none of this matters. Within a year of meeting him, Old Lass has packed up our Wendywood lives and moved us to a new home.

The house is pretty and big and not at all like our Wendywood flat. Plonked in the middle of a Parkhurst road lined by trees, the path beyond the heavy wooden gate leads through the garden and up three steps to the veranda. The house is painted white. A fresh, deep, chalky white that fails absolutely in concealing the elderly cracks recently painted over. Arranged starkly on the white veranda are two of Second Husband's antique chairs. They are brown and wooden – as is all the furniture in this house. The back garden homes the most gloriously big oak tree, under which Old Lass will later get married, as well as a pergola happily drowning under grapevines, the only Greek whisper in our new home. Protector & Soul and I hate the place.

Nonetheless, we set about making our new, shared bedroom as 'us' as we possibly can. Our wooden bunk beds, painted a light lavender, are placed against a wall, leaving us more room than we knew what to do with. The parquet floors are streaked with fresh damage as we push the other furniture around from one spot to the next. We know from the second we move in that we will be confined to our bedroom most of the time. Second Husband, when he isn't in his dark and gloomy antique shop a few roads away, lies on the old daybed that serves as a couch in the lounge. No matter the time of day or the state of the weather, whenever he is at home he draws closed the heavy green-and-red velvet curtains, blocking the outside world from dancing across the screen on which the History Channel flickers. Old Lass brings him beers. Old Lass makes him bacon pasta. Second Husband stinks and stains the velvet curtains and daybed cushions and air with plumes of blue Peter Stuyvesant smoke. Old Lass rolls joints for the two of them to smoke in the garden. Second Husband returns to the couch, is brought another beer and resents Old Lass for having children who follow her from home to house. Instead of asking us how we are, Old Lass tells my sister and me to 'keep it down'.

One day, a huge bakkie arrives and dumps piles of gravel in the front garden. Men begin raking it over the soft grass and bare earth. I am horrified by the knowledge of an impending torture on my always-bare soles. Other than my shared bedroom, the garden is my only playroom. Gravel on the outside, eggshells on the inside. My nightmarish preoccupation with stones in shoes being fully realised and leaned into.

So it is that Protector & Soul and I begin retreating further and further from Old Lass. It comes easily to us.

Second weekends insist on continuing, and off Protector & Soul and I go to My Father's house. When we arrive, he asks about Second Husband. We tell him we don't like him. He asks us why. We tell him, 'We just don't.' We are children and we don't know how to say, 'It's actually just quite crap having to share our mother, who is our favourite person.' Or perhaps, 'We can feel it in our bones that he doesn't want us around and that he's angry Mom has us.' We are children and we don't even know that this is our reasoning. My Father asks us about Old Lass.

Is she still going into the garden to smoke?

Yes.

What is she smoking?

We don't know.

Are they normal cigarettes from the blue box with the camel on it that she usually smokes, or is it a cigarette that she has rolled and filled with dried green grass?

Both. None. We don't know.

My Father then instructs us to search through the garden in Second Husband's house when we return after school on Monday.

Collect the little ends of the cigarettes, you know, the stompies. Hide them away somewhere in your room and bring them to me the next time you come here.

And so we do.

When we return home to the Parkhurst house at the end of the weekend, Protector & Soul and I start sorting through the tiny, ornate boxes strewn around our bedroom that until now have had no function. Too tiny to put anything other than Christmas beetles into, which I had done a few weeks before with the intention of acquiring new pets. When I open the lid to take out my new companions hours after capturing them the first day, one has died and the other falls into my mushy palm and begins scratching away at my chubby flesh with its spiky legs. Disgusted by how they've turned on me, I toss them immediately, corpse and ungrateful asshole, into a bush in the garden. Thus solidifying my lifelong hatred for the little creatures.

Repurposing the beetle coffin, we make sure Old Lass and Second Husband are nowhere to be found before heading into the garden, our eyes glued to the ground.

Within minutes of our dark eyes adjusting to the sun absorbing and reflecting the grey gravel, we find the little end of a joint. The *stompie* thing. The rolled cardboard tip still securely held in place by determined saliva, we pop our evidence into my little box and run into our bedroom. Little hiding places everywhere. A box within a jewellery box within a music box on which a plastic ballerina dances. Filled with dread and a sense of accomplishment, we wait and wait for the next weekend we'll spend with My Father.

At this point, my sister has already been forced to flourish into a warrior. As though her interior resilience is leaking through her pores, each year she requests combat boots, action man figurines and remote-controlled cars for her birthday. I, a living, breathing floral pattern wrapped in a bow, serve as her confidante, shadow and contrast. Father's Friday arrives before we know it. Again, our weekend bags sit in our classrooms stuffed with pyjamas, clothes to play in, remote controls struggling against zips, and a little box in which the remnants of one of our mother's joints lies, still, holding its breath. Our entire lives packed into bags, between two homes, neither of which we want to exist in.

We hand the little plastic box, which we have wrapped in toilet paper, to My Father.

This stuff smells so bad, sissie.

He tells us what a good job we've done.

Days at My Father's house consist of watching TV, asking our YiaYia to make us waffles and playing with our cousins. On rare occasions, My Father comes into the garden and sits with crossed legs in the middle of the lawn. Protector & Soul and I sprint past, close enough for him to grab our ankles. This is the entire game. Trying to run fast enough to avoid being caught, being caught and dragged to the ground and being tickled. When the evenings come, My Father puts on a movie in his small, childhood bedroom, which is now his tiny, adulthood bedroom, and Protector & Soul and I fight over who gets to lie next to him on his single bed – the alternative being a small mattress placed on the floor. He lies on the bed with one of us in his arms, wearing his thin cotton sleep shorts and nothing else. When it is my turn, I lie on his chest and twirl my finger through the hairs, breathing in his smell. But just as I get comfortable, I immediately regret fighting for this prize, resenting this thing resembling comfort in the very instant I receive it.

Everything is sour. The single bed, his smell, his chest hair. As we grow, my sister and I fight over who gets to lie on the mattress on the floor. Eventually, we unite and come up with explanations as to why we should *both* lie together on the mattress on the floor, leaving My Father with more room to himself on the bed. When My Father is elsewhere in the house, Protector & Soul and I are both drawn to and repelled by the decorations and odds and ends lying openly on the white shelf that runs alongside the bed.

Porn magazines turned inwards on themselves reveal plump tits, all either too hard or too soft. Furry pussies form the top of the pyramids that have been turned on their heads. Condom wrappers, some with tenants, some without, poke out from between books while others brazenly bask in the glow of the bedroom's exposed light bulb. *Call Girl* catalogues line up behind ashtrays and worry beads from Greece.

One night when my explanations have failed to convince him that I should keep my distance, I lie next to him on the bed. I am six years old. He touches his index finger down on the raised mole that sits directly in the centre of my chest between my 10-cent nipples.

'One day when you have boobs, men will love kissing you right here on this mole, Mouse,' he tells me as he taps his finger on it a few more times.

Perhaps storytelling runs in our blood, because when we go off to our own bedroom at My Father's house, my sister and I beg him to tell us stories of his childhood before we crash into sleep. Maybe we are just looking for some semblance of normality, a fantasy. I am desperate to picture him as a young boy, as someone I can relate to fully. As someone who is other than My Father. We screech for retell requests of stories he's run out of long ago. Tell us again, Dad. This time make it even better. He tells us about how he and his best friend, who'd lived next door to each other since birth, would attach a long piece of string to cans and whisper along it from window to window late at night. He tells us about the mischief and retaliation he'd get up to at school when the pesky Jews who made up the majority of the Parktown Boys' population would tease him, chanting 'Chili willy' unimaginatively. He tells us about peeking through windows that exposed the neighbourhood girls, about running carelessly through quiet streets, about bunking school. Endless tales of being a child, being a child, being a child.

One day, when he and I are alone, My Father tells me about when a grown-up touched his penis when he was a kid.

'I was six years old, just like you are now. I told your YiaYia and your Pappou. No one believed me.'

No one believed me.

No one believed me.

No one believed me.

No one believed me.

It doesn't happen often, but sometimes My Father remembers a story he hasn't told before. When they reveal themselves to him, he tells them immediately. I am six or eight or fourteen and I am told everything by him.

When I used to go to Hillbrow, I'd meet a lot of people you should never meet. Women who trade their bodies as currency. Men who encourage it. One night, a prostitute I knew followed me back home to Rosebank. She used to be beautiful. I was already in the house when she arrived, and she kept ringing the doorbell. I was high, and she wouldn't stop ringing it and ringing it. I got one of my guns from the safe in my bedroom and sat down on the carpeted floor. She sat down on the floor of the patio opposite me on the other side of the door. You know the warped glass in the doors in my house? Yes, so I could see her through that. She sat there crying and begging me for crack. She said I could have her if I'd share. I

*sat there staring at her with a gun in my lap, hoping your YiaYia
wouldn't wake up. I don't know how long we both sat there. But
I just stared at her. And I started to laugh so much. She was so
desperate. I just sat there with my gun, laughing while she begged.*

A few weeks after delivering proof of my mom's vice to My Father,
a woman from Social Services arrives at the Parkhurst house to
check up on me and my sister. Old Lass is hysterical.

Why are you here?
What has that fucker done now?
Whatever he's said isn't true.
He's the addict ... I am not the addict.
My daughters are okay.
Where did you get that?
That's not mine.
It's their father you should be worrying about.

I am too young to be included in any of these conversations.
Protector & Soul is taken into our bedroom alone with the Social
Services lady and I am told to wait outside with my mess of a
mother.

My sister blocks this interaction from her mind within the time
it takes for the woman in the grey pantsuit to climb back into her
car and drive away. She can't tell my mom what was discussed,
staring blankly at Old Lass as she begs for details. Now, all these
years later, Protector & Soul tells me that she can't fill me in on
what was said, not because she doesn't want to, but because her
cells won't even allow her to remember.

'Christy, I don't even know if it was a man or a woman who
came and if it wasn't for you and Mom reminding me of this
altogether, I never would have thought of it again.'

In the greater scheme of things, nothing ever comes of this visit.
Nevertheless Old Lass is furious with My Father. She is especially
furious with us after we inform her, screaming, that we'd only
done what My Father told us to do by collecting *her* stompie.

*Do you know how much trouble this could have gotten me
into?*

36

But Dad says what you do is illegal, so why do you do it?
I am not the addict – your father is the addict.

At this, Protector & Soul and I screech, wail, despise Old Lass openly.

He is not an addict!
We love going to his house!
He doesn't do bad things any more!
YiaYia is there too!
We were helping you by giving him the green tobacco cigarette!

We have been trained so well. We believe every word My Father has said.

He clings to the warped notion that he should get full custody of us with such fervour that he recruits us as his soldiers in a war against our mother. He wants us all to himself and the more he fights to keep us, the more Old Lass feigns tightening the reins on us. Not enough to stop us from going to him every second weekend, but enough to buy us our first ever cellphones so we can contact her if we need to while we're away.

We return home to Old Lass after one such weekend, and our cellphones do not return with us. She questions us, shouting in sadness, desperate for us to actually tell the truth for once, and my head swims. My knees are weak. I am so confused and broken.

A few days earlier, I stand in front of My Father, head swimming, knees weak, confused and sobbing, as he demands I give him my new Nokia. He goes out alone that night. Our cellphones take our places on his visit to Hillbrow. He smokes them when he gets home.

Things deteriorate with furious speed in the home we now creep through in Parkhurst. The house that clearly belongs to Second Husband. Here, Old Lass learns how to ignore hearing things and how to unhear them altogether. Second Husband moves hatefully through the halls and over the floors. One summer's day, Protector & Soul is reading *Harry Potter* on a distressed, white-wicker couch that has found a home on the veranda among its wooden comrades. Second Husband arrives home in his white bakkie, and before even having manoeuvred his body out of the car, he yells at her for not greeting him in his own home, for being disrespectful, for existing.

Old Lass says nothing. Protector & Soul gets up and joins me in our bedroom where she casually continues to read.

'I just never read books outside again,' she tells me now.

Second Husband makes an incredibly easy target of himself. Between the stink of his cologne trailing behind him through the house, leaving us wrinkling our noses and pretending – with much exaggeration – to dry-heave, to the way he speaks to Old Lass as though she is undeserving of any semblance of love.

He speaks in the way that I now recognise as an adult, a way that keeps certain women going back to awful men. Like shoes that we insist on wearing only because they feel so good once they've been taken off. So Old Lass stays, wilting at a rare kind word that slips from a nasty mouth every few days.

His grip over the house and its three inhabitants tightens. Protector & Soul and I aren't allowed to eat his food or drink his drinks or breathe in his oxygen or cough within his earshot. Hating him is as easy as loving our mother.

And so we forget My Father's indiscretions with a graceful ease as we thrill him with the stories of Second Husband's instead. Soon, we became spies instead of nuisances in the Parkhurst home. Upon hearing about Second Husband's plan to take Old Lass and us away to Mozambique on a school holiday, My Father instructs Protector & Soul to steal his passport. Now, at 26 years of age, my sister's mind draws welcome and infuriating blanks.

'I remember being told by Dad to steal it. I remember waiting until Second Husband left the house and going through his cupboards. I remember finding the passport. I don't remember taking it or giving it to Dad. But I must have, because a few days later it was discovered missing.'

One day not long after our Mozambican trip is cancelled due to the curious case of the missing passport, Old Lass is standing over the stove boiling pasta and melting butter. Her two friends Eugene and Nathan sit at the long, narrow wooden table that runs down the centre of the kitchen, tossing back drinks with Second

Husband and waiting for the pasta to be placed in front of them and fatten them up. The three men discuss relationships and marriage, not children.

Second Husband glances in my mother's direction and says to her back, 'So ... should we do this thing?'

'What thing?' she asks, pouring the strained penne into the scorching butter that has singed a nutty brown.

'Get married.'

'Yes.'

To say my sister and I are devastated is an understatement. On this occasion of protest, as with those that have preceded it, Old Lass reminds us how lucky we are to have Second Husband. Because of him, we have food in our belly and a roof over our heads. We are children. No one has explained to us that the Splodge Shop is barely making any money, flower soaps and textured pillows failing to bring home the big bucks. We are children. No one has explained to us that sometimes you have to bite your tongue and walk on eggshells and betray your children and climb into bed with horrendous men because you need a roof over your head and food in your belly, to 'protect' the very kids who now resent you because of it.

The wedding day arrives and Protector & Soul and I argue with Old Lass. We insist on wearing jeans. *I* insist on wearing jeans. We are determined to don the least celebratory outfits we can find. Jeans don't say, *Good job, Old Lass*; jeans say, *Go fuck yourself, Soon-to-be-stepdad*. Old Lass is gentle. Even at her hardest she is one of the gentlest souls. After tiresome negotiations, I trade in my jeans for a grey skirt with denim trim and try to be furious with her, but on this day she is more breathtaking than ever. I stare at her and devour the sight of her fingers, the fat knuckles we've all inherited, and her ankles, tanned and slender, and her eyes, the black beads brought to attention by her black hair, as though the universe has gifted them to me. I count my blessings, knowing even at such a young age to look at my grown-up mother as a crystal ball, a gateway to the features, wrinkles, figure and hairline that await me. In this, I am smug, often revelling for hours in how exquisite my mother is compared to some of the ugly moms my friends have been stuck with. Old Lass pulls a cream-coloured lace leotard over her midnight hair, which falls freely, the tips just grazing the top of her tiny boobs. She snaps shut the three metal buttons of the bodysuit between her thighs, does the same to the three buttons that secure the leotard at her caramel neck, before stepping into a floor-length skirt that on any other woman would look like a repurposed gold bedspread embroidered with flowers rather than a boutique dream. On my mother it looks magnificent.

After Old Lass and Second Husband say their vows under the oak tree in front of the forty-or-so family members and friends serving as tipsy witnesses, the photographer asks for photos of the newly married couple and their children. Old Lass sits on a bench next to her sickly sweet husband. Protector & Soul and I sit on either end of them, and Second Husband's two daughters – who until this point I've been ferociously pretending don't exist – squeeze themselves into the shot.

This is the first time Second Husband has ever embraced me in any way, I note as he slings his arm over my shoulder for the photo. Without meaning to, I feel a joy boiling up inside of me. I consider how happy my beautiful mother looks. Her smile is so big its claws are tugging at the corners of her eyes. Her energy is so light, limitlessly loving. Maybe the wedding will change everything, I think under the foreign but welcomed weight of Second Husband's arm. I begin to burst with hope and feelings of guilt, as though I am abandoning my sister on an island of resentment, pushing myself from our shared shore on a raft of forgetfulness, to the horizon of forgiveness, leaving her rubbing sticks together, all the better to burn that whole fucking place down, alone, behind me.

Click. The photographer turns his back to go and take pictures of the other guests. The instant Second Husband realises the lens is no longer on us, he rips his arm from behind me and stalks off to get a drink. My face falls, skinny chicken arms ache as I turn my raft around and paddle with everything I have to join my sister on the island of hate; she, thankfully, hasn't noticed I'd left.

Old Lass and her freshly acquired husband flit off to Mauritius a few days after the wedding. My sister and I are forced to stand with Step Sisters 1 and 2 on the pavement outside (which too has been covered in gravel), to wave them off as they leave for the airport. As though recreating a precious and nauseatingly happy scene from a romantic comedy, they turn their heads back at us, waving at their children and their new children as they peel off. Before they've turned the corner, I decide I've had quite enough of this waving business, and lower my arm. Step Sister 1 grabs my arm, hoists it into the air and insists I wave until their car is completely out of sight.

Life for Protector & Soul and me is uneventful. Not as though nothing is happening; we're just used to what is happening. We're used to going to school where I have one friend and my sister has two. My friend is a girl named Alexia, a squishy and uninhibited Cypriot with whom I bond through tears on the first day of Grade 1. My sister's two friends are me and Alexia. I am used to stealing the Slim Slabs from Alexia's lunchbox and giving her half my sandwich in exchange. Not because I want the Slim Slab – no one ever actually wants the Slim Slab – but because I am sad she's been given the Slim Slab in her lunchbox in the first place. 'It's because I have all this puppy fat,' she tells me as she grabs at her fleshy, dimpled side with her index finger and thumb, just as her mom has taught her to do. 'Also, I'm pre-diabetic,' she says, hungrily chewing on her sandwich ration.

I am used to being told I'm going to fail. I am used to Protector & Soul pushing people down the concrete grandstand with all the force she can muster as she defends my honour. I am used to picking fights and using my big, pushing, warrior sister as a threat. We are used to going home and straight to our bedroom. We are used to our new life, just as Old Lass is used to hers. She continues to bring Second Husband beers, to roll joints, to light joints, to now rid the garden and house of any evidence of the smoked joints. We are used to the way Second Husband shouts at our mother, at the dogs and at us.

One day we're in the kitchen and he kicks a dog belonging to one of his friends who is away on a vacation and I scream.

I scream at him to stop, I scream at Old Lass to give a fuck that her husband has just kicked a creature that is now in pain, tail between its legs, black-and-white torso crumpled in on itself lying on the threshold of the kitchen door that leads to the back garden. I decide people who kick black-and-white dogs, people who kick any dogs, are the worst people of all.

CHAPTER 7

Why Does My Body Insist?

I am used to packing my bag. I am used to going to My Father's house. To eating waffles washed down with sweet tea. To running through the carpeted halls at night. To running through the garden in the day and being caught and tickled and hating myself for laughing.

Why do children do that? Why can't we help but laugh even when we hate being tickled? Why do we still laugh even when the tears are bubbling up, sobs of anguish buried under blasts of laughter. Why is the laughter always louder than the pleas for it to stop? Why don't the adults stop tickling us when we say, please stop tickling me? Instead I am told by My Father, 'Tell me you love me and then I'll stop.' And so I laugh my regrettable laugh and cry my sincere tears and spit, 'Okay, I love you, I love you' through gritted teeth and I hate this and when it stops I am so relieved I say, 'Thank you.'

At 14 years of age, I reply, 'Thank you ... Yes, they're real, but I'm actually 14,' when a 40-year-old man asks me where I got my boob job done because he wants his girlfriend's tits to look just as good as mine.

At 16, I still greet with a smile the boy who tells everyone I gave him a blow job behind the Jolly Roger.

When I am a 19-year-old waitress I say, 'I appreciate the compliment but please don't touch my ass again,' when a drunk tries to finger me through my thin, black cotton leggings as I walk past.

When I'm 22 I tell my boyfriend, 'Thank you. I like it when you slap me during sex but maybe next time please don't be so rough without us having established a safe word beforehand.'

In each of my 23 years I feel the need to preface a 'No' to a man with a declaration of love and gratitude.

Angrier than I am with My Father, I am angry with me. Why does my body insist on convulsing in laughter when I despise being tickled? Why don't adults stop when we beg them to? Why do I keep lying on my belly and pushing my vagina into my cupped hands and why does it feel so good? Why does my little, convulsing body feel so good? Why don't I stop? Why do I feel naughty for doing it next to my sister in bed before we go to sleep? Why do I feel less guilty doing it next to My Father while the movie plays on the TV? How do I know that this thing I've been doing since I was four years old is kinda bad even though it feels so good, even though no one has actually told me it is bad?

I've been masturbating furiously for as long as I can remember. Lying on my belly, my vagina either moulded to the shape of my cupped hands or my hands moulded to the mound of my vagina. Either way, it's been a goddamn terrifying match made in heaven.

I've heard children who start masturbating from a young age are more intelligent than their self-sexless counterparts. I don't know if I believe that. Sometimes I think it was the S.E.X. conversation with My Father, the magazines erecting naked women into my consciousness, the mole on my chest that led me into a sweaty frenzy at such a young age. I think of these things and sometimes I believe them to be the cause, and sometimes I don't.

As an adult I am hit across the face with the shell of an Italian palm, I see stars, I am choked, I come to, to see stars, I say, 'Hurt me more.' Sometimes I think of these things and other times I don't. I consider my sinister palms and bruised mound and raw cheek and I consider the purity and absurdity, the necessity and the unbelonging of all these things. I masturbate furiously until I pass out in exhaustion, regardless of my age or my head space, until my teeth have been clenched so hard they feel raw – worse than they feel when I smoke cigarettes on an empty stomach. I touch and push and insist on myself until I am nauseous and dehydrated, perching on the toilet dying for a wee and willing my swelling to go down to allow me as much. I do everything I do with a sense of urgency. I do it as though it is the last time I'll ever be able to. I use it as an opportunity to rehearse for the next time.

One day, Second Husband brings home a tiny Jack Russell. She is fragile and pretty and looks as though she's swallowed a stress ball. She has a single brown dot on top of her head. She is fabulously round. She is the family's new dog, but in the moment I see her, I know she is actually my new best friend. Second Husband suggests we name her Amelia, and I tell him that that is a stupid name for a dog. I suggest Meila, and so she is. I hold my new friend, and thank Second Husband while whispering under my breath, into my chest, 'I'll never let him kick you, Meila.' The fucker had finally done something right.

CHAPTER 8

Run, Valentia, Run

Only a year into their marriage, Old Lass decides to leave Second
Husband. I don't remember the conversation she must have had
with Protector & Soul and me about it. I can only guess at the
elation in our eyes, egging her on to finish her sentence as she said
it. I know it came after an evening in which Old Lass and Second
Husband fought so viciously that Protector & Soul and I called
My Father. We called the madman to come restore order, and so
he showed up with a hitman name Justin. Justin had a baseball bat
and he and My Father both had guns and everyone was threatened
with death and I was frightened to death. That night, my tummy
ballooned. It ached as it grew and stretched and I could feel my
colon turning spastic and my bowel becoming irritable. That night,
the distress I felt finally found a place to settle, to expand, to make
itself known.

Soon, my sister, mother and I are unpacking boxes in a bedroom
in a small garden cottage on someone's property on a shady road
in a less fancy and far more pleasant suburb than the one we'd just
left. As I unpack, I thank Old Lass again and again for giving my
sister and me the bigger room to share. She pushes the chest into
which old linen will soon be packed and forgotten about around
the tiny square room in a real-life game of Tetris. I thank her again
on top of the last again, and tell her again how badly I feel that she

is getting the small room with the barely-there window offering a view of a brick wall, while we get the airy one with the view of the green. She tells me not to worry. But I do. I am trying to reward her for doing the right thing, the hardest thing, by leaving her husband. I am thrilled by the new bedroom I am to share with my sister, but I also resent it. I want Old Lass to have the view and the air and the space.

What if she hates the small bedroom so much that she makes us go back to Parkhurst where she can see bumblebees dancing on the purple blossoms of the potato bush outside her old bedroom window?

She insists we take the big room.

When I think of this cottage now, this home, I can taste chicken pie on my tongue, on each bud. A warmth rushes to my legs, my shoulders, my cheeks. I am nine years old and I am sitting in front of the gas heater built into the wall. On TV there's a show in which a tribe of children attempt to survive in a world where all the adults have died. Wiped out, all gone. I peel puff pastry, flake by flake, from my slice of Woolworths chicken pie, laying each piece on my wet, patient tongue before letting it melt against my palate, and I ache in my soul for the children who are without parents. Not the real ones, the ones on street corners just roads away from where I sit. I haven't exactly considered those yet. But for the ones inside my TV, my heart bleeds. I count my blessings. My big sister, already toasty warm, has absconded from her spot on the wooden floor in front of the heater and has folded herself into a ball in the corner of the couch. Old Lass, never one to sit still or to make it through an episode of anything without falling asleep, her head gently falling backwards, her mouth an unsealed envelope from which shallow snores escape, avoids a fate in which her children attempt to throw little things into her slit of an open mouth by faffing in the kitchen. Faffing in her bedroom, interrogating her pores in the bathroom mirror, offering us more pie. Antsy and anxious, as always. She is so busy being busy that she doesn't notice her growing nausea.

Meila is balled up as her belly insists she be, in my crossed legs.

47

I run my fingers along her body and feel the fire of the heater in her fur. I place one hand behind me on the floor to lever my body as I slide my bum backwards, legs still crossed, trying not to wake her while I avoid setting her alight.

One blessing sister, one blessing mother, one blessing chicken pie. It's just like Wendywood, except better, because one blessing Meila.

It takes Protector & Soul and me some time to start cultivating our mischievousness. Starting from scratch, we have to rebuild the personalities and quirks of which the Parkhurst house had robbed us. The first few weeks in the cottage, we creep as lightly as we can from room to room. I slink out from my new bedroom and peer around the corner into the kitchen before I realise that I am allowed to breathe again. I march into the kitchen, swing open the fridge, and revel in the shelves. Stocked with yoghurt and Coca-Cola and cheese and tomatoes and the makings of an exceptional sandwich, I feel like the luckiest girl in the world.

After school every day, Old Lass drops us off at the cottage before heading back to the Splodge Shop, so a woman named Valentia is hired as a domestic worker, nanny and form of entertainment (although she and our mom aren't aware of this last function, one bestowed upon her by my sister and me). Valentia is impossibly round and full. She smiles broadly, sincerely, greeting us cheerfully when we get home. We like her immediately. We realise quickly, however, how little it takes to tip her temperament in the other direction. She is big and bossy but we are getting braver by the day. We begin to play tricks on her. One day, Protector & Soul and I are in the kitchen while Valentia cleans the bathroom at the other end of the cottage. My sister silently gestures for me to follow her as she opens the door of the pantry. We climb in, stifling our giggles, and quietly shut the door behind us. Protector & Soul cracks open the thin, wooden pantry door, and shouts 'Valentia' in such a way that her voice scatters. It shoots from her mouth and reverberates off the opposite wall. It perches atop the curtain rod and sinks into the couch cushions. It swims through the lounge, takes a sharp right down the hallway and eventually lands in

Valentia's ear. By the time V rounds the corner, the remnants of the yell are everywhere. It is untraceable now in the stillness.

'Yes, what? Where are you?'

We stand still as corpses, our hands pressed over our mouths to smother our sniggers. We watch her shadow pass over the narrow crack of the imperfectly designed pantry and we hold our breath.

She walks through the open-plan space as briskly as her chunky thighs allow, and peers behind the kitchen counter where we should be sitting and doing our homework. She goes to the lounge window and looks out, but there is nothing other than the crispy brown grass of the lawn and the homeowner's bull terriers behind gates on the other end, itching and pacing to get out. She walks through the kitchen and stops right outside the pale brown door we're hiding behind. Protector & Soul slaps my hand gently to stop me from fiddling with the biscuit packet I reached for in a moment of boredom.

Eventually, she gives up. We hear her sigh in irritation and return to the bathroom. Once everything is still again, silent except for the sound of a wet rag wiping down the porcelain of the bathtub, I open the door a crack, round my lips into a fleshy megaphone and shout, 'Valentia!' before retreating once again into the dark, salty pantry.

Meila becomes a hostage in this house, but it's our only option. The landlord's bull terriers have taken to eyeing her as though she's a plump snack. The homeowner insists they're timid and friendly, but one look at their tapered snouts and tiny, slanted eyes assures me they're assholes. One day, curious Meila escapes from the cottage without us noticing. Silently, her short legs carry her across the lawn, the grass tickling her soft, spotted belly as she goes. It's not until we hear barking, raging, silence, deafening, that our heads spin wildly in the direction of our puppy's usual hiding spots. She isn't sitting in the corner of the lounge. She isn't snoozing, her head hidden in the school bags we've left unzipped and strewn around the dining room. She isn't munching mouthfuls from her bowl in the kitchen. She is taken in, snapped up, in the jaws of one of the dogs at the far end of the garden. She is squealing. Her neck is being chewed into, held in place, while Asshole 1 takes a bite out of her fleshy stomach. By the time we've sprinted, already sobbing, over the lawn and to the gate through which Meila has easily squeezed herself in an effort to make new friends, there is bright red blood everywhere. We screech for someone from the main house to open the gate, and from its depths someone clicks a button, bringing the heavy metal gate to lazy life. It slides open slowly, unaffected by the blood splatters running down its slats. Old Lass knows to never get in the middle of a dog fight – in this case, an unrequited death match – but she throws herself in anyway. She knows not to take hold of Meila and pull and pull, kicking the air around the mean dogs as a swooshing warning, but she does anyway.

When Old Lass has Meila cradled in her arms and out of the mouths, red and quivering, eyelids showing glimpses of both this reality and the other, we jump into our mother's malachite-green City Golf and tear up Johannesburg's roads on our way to the vet.

Meila survives, is stitched together again sans a chunk of belly here and a piece of neck there, and we take her home to the source of her horror. The apologetic landlord has cable-tied plastic to the bottom portion of the gate, just high enough to keep Meila out and low enough to afford Assholes 1 and 2 a view of the outside world.

Valentia dotes on us, dotes on the almost-dead Meila, tells me to get myself my own damn glass of water. One weekday afternoon, she is leaving to go home and asks an impatient child to open the main gate of the property. I stand at the front door tapping my bare, brown foot. I press the button that opens the heavy gate. She walks so slowly I fume. I wonder whether she's doing this on purpose. Whether she takes her sweet time now because she's resentful of having spent so many hours dedicated to us. To a home where agitated girls blast Eminem, a home with an injured dog needing constant attention, a cottage sealed tightly from the outside world and the asshole bull terriers, stiflingly stuffy and refusing a breeze.

My finger hovers over the button of the automatic gate as I consider everything and nothing; I am furious, despite having nothing better to do. Before Valentia is even halfway across the lawn where her sweet escape awaits her, I plummet my finger down and press hard, sending the gate lurching closed. Seeing the senseless gate nearing a complete close, Valentia begins to run, her bags swatting her hips as her curves send them into orbit, bringing them crashing down into her once again. And so a new game is born. The next day Protector & Soul and I stand, fingers hovering together, mastering the timing, watching Valentia run.

During these winter months in the cottage, all dinners are eaten from in front of the gas heater or the comfort of the couch. I am starting to look like chicken pie, and Meila is healing. One day after work, Old Lass asks Protector & Soul and me to please sit at the glass dining table. We immediately know something is wrong.

'I'm pregnant,' Old Lass tells us blankly ... and I am both heartbroken and elated. I love small things. Puppies, babies, Christmas beetles until they turn on you. But I hate what this baby means; it means it has a father.

We ask Old Lass for confirmation that it is indeed Second Husband's baby growing inside her toned belly.

'Obviously, girls.'

Does this mean we have to go live with him again?

'Yes ... But I promise this time will be different now that there's a baby.'

So my sister and I pack up our lives, we cry, we are heartbroken, we are joyous, we have a little sibling on the way, we are Eminem's number-one fans. We're asked to keep it down while we pack, not because we're disturbing in our existence, but because Eminem is disturbing when bolstered by such furious volume. We can feel in our Greek bones that our entire lives are about to change, again. I can feel the puff pastry fading from my tongue's memory, I can see in my mind's eye the stocked fridge shelves I will once again be forbidden to touch, I can smell the stale Stuyvesant of Second Husband's breath and I am coaching my voice on how to return to a whisper.

51

A few days before we leave the cottage to continue with our old and new life, Protector & Soul storms into the lounge where I am sitting on the floor, surrounded by boxes and playing with dolls.

'Christy, we're not listening to Eminem any more. In one of his songs he talks about putting a woman's tampon in poison so it kills her from the inside out. We're feminists now.'

'Okay!' I say with a conviction matching that of my big sister, while I rack my brain for the meanings of these things 'tampons' and 'feminists'.

CHAPTER 9

The Ready-to-Burst Blue House

In the months since Old Lass left him, Second Husband has moved to another house a few streets away from the one in which he'd married my mother. By the time we return to him – one glowing, growing woman and her two sad children – he has barely started unpacking his own boxes. This house, Parkhurst 2, has four bedrooms and a spacious, airy garden cottage. It's painted a light blue that is so bright it's offensive to the clear sky that parades a few wispy, white clouds above us.

As Protector & Soul and I enter, Old Lass tells us to go pick out a bedroom each. We're fucking livid about having to share a home with this man again but, dear god, we're each getting our own room for the first time in our lives. My 11-year-old sister is ecstatic, throwing her head into this room and the next, bouncing from side to side along the shared hallway from which our three options sprout. Second Husband joins us in the hallway, figures out what's going on, and begins to laugh deeply and from within his belly, shaking his sunken head while he does so.

'No, no … You get the bedroom at the end of the hall. Until the baby is born, Step Sister 1 and Step Sister 2 each get their own bedroom for when they come visit, so you two have to share.'

Old Lass shouts at her husband, shouts her apologies at us, shouts that his children barely even visit him and it isn't fair, shouts that he promised it would be different this time. But nothing ever comes of it, all this shouting.

Second Husband's right arm is made to dismiss people. Rising like a Mexican wave, rolling from the ball of his shoulder, it languidly propels his hand, snaps his wrist, flicking his palm upwards and into my mother's eyeshot, right in front of her tense face. A shoulder, an arm, a hand, a wrist, a palm, a fluid gesture to remind his wife that she isn't even worth the conversation, breath wasted on anything other than inhaling through his nose while the bum of a Heineken bottle kisses the sky.

We continue to go to My Father's house on second weekends while our mom's tummy grows. He continues to insist on being dead to the world for two days at a time, begrudgingly sweating drugs out of his system through his clear pores, for even at his worst – even when he can't afford his pain and his cure – he is never without his Clinique. When he comes to, he wants Protector & Soul and me to prepare mentally for a sibling who will be born a 'retard'. As Old Lass continues to roll and light and smoke joints during every day of her pregnancy, so my sister and I begin to pray. I hadn't prayed since I realised that the universe refuses to gift me a summer's snow. I gave up years ago in defiance. It's something silly that six-year-olds do, begging for freebies and impossible joys from a man in the clouds. But now I am nine and more grown up and I am rediscovering the desperation of muttering words under my breath, chanting mantras in my mind, screaming sobs and pleas into my pillow.

Please don't let my brother or sister be a retard.

Please make Mom not want to smoke any more.

Please don't let the baby come out wanting drugs.

Does weed make a baby addicted? Must remember to ask sissie.

No, focus …

Please God, let me have a normal sibling.

But PS: Even if they're not normal, I promise I'll take care of them and love them anyway.

With the last wish, my mind begins to draw a round face, etching in small eyes, on the inside of my closed eyelids. I don't know what weed babies look like, so I conjure up images of Downs children. I quietly consider the last person I saw with Down Syndrome, at a fun day at my primary school months earlier. Candyfloss was spun, delicately wrapped around long sticks from a yellow machine that whizzed and cast the air around it in a sugar glow. A few wise children stood, tongues out in the November air, catching sweet particles. Inflatable slides were slid down, sending hotdogs back up children's throats. Heads tentatively bobbed into tubs with warm water and warm apples riddled with unfamiliar bite marks. Speakers as big as stubby men were placed all over. From them, the notes of Celine Dion rose and plummeted around us before making way for the crooning of Alanis Morissette. I directed a stink eye in the direction of the swarm of peers who had now gathered, pink and blue and green tongues held to the heavens as they caught sweetness on their buds. I found them foolish for doing only what everyone else was doing and I envied them for having got a spot in the sugar mist while there was still time. While I cursed my comrades and considered a career in singing one day, I saw that the crowd passing through the nearest quad was beginning to avoid an obstacle of some kind. Groups of people moved mindlessly through the bare, brown-bricked courtyard lined by hallways and classrooms and then they hesitated. Their eyes were drawn downwards before shooting back up and staring blankly and forcefully straight in front of them. Mothers tugged at their children's T-shirts and pulled them to the outskirts of the pulsating crowd. People walked, hesitated, glanced down, forced their eyes up, and yanked their children into the quarantine of obliviousness offered by a change in direction.

I moved in closer. I saw a girl lying on her side on the warm, dirty bricks. She was by all appearances imagining a mermaid's tail where her thick, heavy legs were, and an otherworldly smile stretched her thin lips wide across her oval face. I felt like I had seen this face before; in fact, I was convinced all Downs children were siblings – their resemblance to one another as uncanny as mine to all the tanned women on my mom's side of the family.

I couldn't bear to look at her, yet couldn't tear my eyes away. She was now, with all her might, heaving her legs, sewn together with a whimsical and invisible thread, sideways and up-up-up, barely two centimetres off the ground. But I swear to god at some point, perhaps on the third or fourth try, her pale, greenish calves come crashing back to earth, snatching up small stones and embedding debris into her soft skin, I began to see it. She was a mermaid. She was sitting on a large rock jutting out of a rough and playful sea, her purple tail moving like fluid, like liquid fucking gold. I saw her thin hair thicken in the ocean breeze and understood the smile on her face, for I was wearing it then too. I was nine years old, old enough to know better than to fall in love with mermaids and dreams and glitter once again. There was glitter falling from the sky – I could see it floating through the air. It was blocking out the view of the grey tuck shop to the left of the mermaid and me, blurring the vision of the curious children and anxious mothers and drunk fathers. It was landing on the mermaid's eyelashes and embedding itself in the middle parting of her hair and was more special and more delicious than the candyfloss wind could ever be. I stood absorbed in the salty air of a faraway seaside, inhaling sparkle when someone bumped into me. I was yanked from the ocean, flung out of the place where everything smells of shells and sand. Boiled viennas were sneaking their disgusting scent up my nostrils once again. My bare feet landed hard, smack on the hot floor of the quad, and I could see the rock and the waves and the glitter being sucked from existence. They vibrated, faster and faster and faster until they began to spin, a colourful vortex of brown and blue and foamy white, speckled with flakes of bursting colour. The vortex disappeared into itself and I raised my head to blink back tears of having seen another world only to be robbed of it. I glanced down at the mermaid.

She was gone. Instead, I saw again the heavy girl with the small eyes lying on her side on the ground. She was gently wiping her hands on her long denim shorts, dislodging tiny pebbles and bits of gravel from her palm. I was heartbroken that it was all over; this dream and gateway and alternate universe that was somehow alerted to my intrusion and swiftly shut down. I waited for the special girl to hoist herself up from the floor and do something in the normal world, but she didn't. Once her palms were clear and comfortable, she brushed off the bricks before laying them flat again. She closed her eyes, and within seconds her ethereal smile had returned to her face.

I consider that a special, weed baby might not be so bad after all. Perhaps there is a wild, edible jungle or herd of unicorns awaiting his arrival, and maybe, if I'm lucky, he'll take me with him to visit sometimes.

The pregnancy is hard on Old Lass. A year before Second Husband plants an unsuspecting seed in her unsuspecting 40-year-old belly, she is diagnosed with diabetes. Her already tiny body has continued to shrink and shrink until she resembles little more than a faint echo of herself. She is weak and dizzy and unwell and then heartbroken and relieved when the diagnoses arrives. For the rest of her life she has to inject herself in her thigh or belly before meals and before bed and after an illegal sweet and after rising to a dangerous, accidental high. Her age and her diabetes make carrying the large baby within her small belly incredibly difficult. Her boobs, a size 32AA (in essence, nipples rising off her chest in a mild curiosity, never adventurous enough to clamber up even the lowest molehill) balloon and continue to balloon until they are sized an inexplicably massive EE. Her belly grows and grows and before we know it, we are told there is a boy growing beneath the stretched, hairy dark skin of her stomach. There is a glow. I see it around her when I spy on her in the mornings, drinking coffee in the garden, her arm perched on the arch of her lower back. There she is, my mother. There they are, my baby brother and my mother, the glowing teapot. Smoke rises out of her mouth like steam from her spout and she is effortlessly graceful – and pissing me off immeasurably. Still, she is my favourite person. Still, I cannot wait for my little friend to arrive.

Second Husband wants to name him Joshua but Old Lass refuses. 'It's too Jewish,' she says. She suggests Terry, and Second Husband refuses. 'I'm not naming my child after your brother.' And so it goes, on and on and on. Jew-ish names, Greek names, painfully white English names flying back on forth. Eventually they settle on a name, on the condition that no one ever refers to him as 'Alex', only by his full name.

I don't care what his name is or how many middle names Second Husband insists on squeezing in between his first and last. To me, he is Stinky.

A few months later, I am now 10 years old and levitating in my school seat. Propelled by anxiety and excitement, my toes don't register the ground. Old Lass is in the hospital to have Stinky cut out of her, what with her high-risk pregnancy and all. Before the office assistant who arrives at the classroom door manages to even utter a word, I am out of my seat and packing up my pencils.

When Protector & Soul and I arrive at the hospital, we bypass our mother, the source of everything, and go straight to the good stuff. The little glass cage where all the new babies are kept. There he is, yellow as fuck, dreaming a jaundice dream, weighing a solid 3.1 kilograms despite being a month premature. His head is huge and round, but in a normal huge and round way. His eyes are little slits, but in a normal the-family-has-roots-in-Asia-Minor-and-we-all-have-slanted-eyes kinda way. He is yellow and squishy and, from what I can tell, he isn't special to anyone at all but us. I fall in love with him instantly without having any idea at all that he is about to save my life.

When he eventually comes home, still yellow, to the bright blue house, he is placed in a small cot under a UV light. I spend my time staring at him. At his heavy head. His flimsy neck. The full thick, brown hair already twirling itself into wispy curls at the base of his neck and his impossibly long eyelashes, which fill me with envy. I was a bald, gremlin baby. I had wrinkles where my eyebrows should have been and pink bows clipped to the few delicate strands of hair Old Lass could grasp, tired as she was of people asking her how old her baby boy was. Here he was, our little Greek god, the features that make for a pretty girl absolutely wasted on him. I begin to search for an olive complexion beneath his jaundice in the hopes that his cells opted for the warm glow of our mother's skin rather than the speckled, pasty flesh of his father. I examine his hands. He has the slender, straight fingers and neat, long nail beds of all the men in my mother's family. I rejoice. I gently place my hand under his left leg and squeeze the area where one day I hope Old Lass's calf muscles will reincarnate themselves beneath his skin. I pull Second Husband's legs into my mind's eye. They have no shape, no curves; there is nothing defining about them. They are a pale bore, and to have one set wandering through the house is more than enough. Only time will tell, I think as I wish him to be more us than he will ever be his father.

CHAPTER 10

A Village of Idiots and Children

A second Friday morning arrives and Protector & Soul and I tell Old Lass that we won't be packing our weekend bags this time round, or any time again. We don't want to go to My Father any more. She asks us why and we tell her that we hate him and we hate being in his house. There, we said it. What I don't tell her is that now that Stinky is home, I don't want him to be without his sisters for two days at a time. He needs an entire village, even if it is a village made up of idiots and children.

Old Lass calls My Father and tells him not to pick us up from school in the afternoon; we won't be going to him this weekend. We are elated and grateful and jump into the car and go to school.

When we return, hours later, to the blue house after being collected by Old Lass, we have barely kicked off our school shoes when we hear screaming from outside the house. The doorbell buzzes, My Father screams. My mom, sister and I walk to the front door; he spots us through the white metal gate and he is insane. I have seen My Father scream so many times in my life. I have seen the sickness in his eyes grow until his entire psyche is lost in fury. I have been enveloped in his rage before, but never like this. He is clutching the rungs of the flimsy white gate and pushing and pulling and tugging and I see the gate straining against itself to remain calm, closed, trying its best to save us from being pummelled with the metal baseball bat he has tucked under his arm.

In moments like these, when My Father is pure monster and nothing resembling a man, his eyes die. They are green and hazel fields that have been shadowed in darkness, until they are black, and they are coming for our souls. His mouth is more dangerous than any bat or gun he's ever threatened us with before. It spits out daggers and bellows a voice that is so deep, so foreign, so demonic.

He pushes and pulls on the gate and screams and screams.

Get into my car right now!

If you don't get into my car right now you are no longer my daughters!

If you don't get into my car right now you are dead to me! Dead! I'll kill you!

You'll be dead to me.

Open this gate.

Get into my car.

You're mine.

You're mine.

You're mine and you're dead to me.

Eventually, he stops pushing and pulling the gate and starts swinging the metal baseball bat at it instead. Old Lass draws my sister and me to her side. This goes on for some time, the banging and the smashing and the swearing and the shouting, before we realise our feet aren't made of lead. That we can run inside the house and slam and bolt the door. But he is a car crash. And there is the relief that comes with Old Lass finally seeing the man she's been sending us to every second weekend.

We sob, we beg him to stop, my belly is pregnant with fear. Eventually he leaves.

We never spend another night in the Rosebank house again, and it's not long before My Father tells us he is going to the mountains in Greece for a few months. To get clean, to come clean to the monks, in the mountains, to collect little blue evil-eye beads to keep the devil away, to bring back blue beads to us, later in life, to protect us from the devil.

Now, I visit the Rosebank house once a week in my least favourite dreams, and on my birthday and name day when YiaYia has baked me kourabiedes and melomakarona. Greek biscuits powdered in icing sugar and doused in honey and nuts. As an adult, I ring the bell of that house, walk through the front door, greet my demons, and melt into my knees.

I don't know how Old Lass pulls it off, but at times – most times – she is both our enemy and our refuge. We feel we deserve so much more from her than we receive, but we couldn't love her more deeply than we already do even if we tried. I suspect many mothers are everything to their children.

She had, after all, birthed the best friendships.

Birthed seeds upon seeds of similarities, of chaos, of resentment.

Black beads for eyes, all the better to scare the boys away.

Fat, hard knuckles.

From YiaYia, to Mama, to me, to future seeds.

Spastic colons, to be able to shit away the panic.

Mutated baby toenails, so that no one sibling was ever tricked into believing they were adopted.

She – the source – brought to the universe the scientist, the lunatic, the opera singer.

Only much later in life do I manage to disable the belief that we must bleed for family. Ache for your mother. Forgive your dying father. Bleed for your blood. Bleed. Bleed. Bleed.

I would then, but I won't now.

I will pulse for my genius, ache for my sanity, revel in my insanity. I will bleed for me and you, for you. Our fat knuckles will toast glasses of wine not because of the resemblance of black eyes, but because the universe insisted we meet, and we choose to stay.

In the chaos of our lives and in the brand-new life of Stinky, Protector & Soul and me, we receive silver linings in the souls of certain people. Our Nona is a life jacket. Hers is the first name on our lips in times of terror.

On a winter night in July, five months after Stinky is born,

Second Husband is filled to the brim with brandy and rage. He locks Old Lass and her three children out of the house. We have no jackets, Stinky is clasped tightly to his mother's chest. Old Lass is a screeching mess, and in moments like this I look at my mother and I am not quite sure whether the embarrassment I see in her hysteria is real or imagined. When she yells at her husband to calm down, I can feel, sewn into her words, her apologies for her children. Sadder than our own situation – children standing on the side of the road locked out of a house – is the fact that this is our mother's reality. We break for her because we see she is heartbroken. There is something about her that welcomes in the men who aim to shatter her. We weep for ourselves, for her. We are furious with her for allowing herself to be treated like this. I try then, as I try in my teens, as I try in my twenties, to put my finger on my mother. To understand why she doesn't see herself clearly.

Is this why she chooses men who are so fucked up?

Does she not want them to see her either?

Who is she hoping will save her?

The man who tried to kill himself with a hot dog topping or the man who sells old furniture and hasn't learnt yet how to thank her for a cup of tea?

What is she waiting for?

Why won't she do better?

Why can't she see herself?

Outside in the cold of that street, we don't have jackets, but I have a phone. I dial Nona's number and whisper to her that we need her.

This time she is in a bubble bath, having returned from an evening out on the town.

'I screamed for your Nono to get into the car, I pulled a tracksuit on, still dripping wet, and we sped to you. When we got there you were shivering. We tried to convince your mom to get into the car and come home with us, but she refused. She wouldn't leave the house after Second Husband let her back in. We brought you and your sister back home, we made you hot chocolate, we told you stories, and we all cried.'

Old Lass breastfeeds Stinky for the appropriate amount of time.
But by the time her boobs start shrivelling into themselves once
again, she is spending every afternoon at her pot dealer, G. He
is quite unlike any man I've ever seen before. He wears colours
in combinations offensive to the eye, but somehow he pulls it
off. Light purples bleed into deep blues on his tie-dye T-shirts.
His cotton pants look as though they've danced their way out
of the sixties and onto his long legs. They are green and orange
and brown and have stars and stripes and moons stitched into
them. Each pair is more outrageous, more ridiculous than the
last. He wears snug, cotton hats that hug the crown of his head.
Old Lass met G through Second Husband, early into dating. The
two men had met in their youth, raised their children together,
smoked pot together. Despite their friendship of countless years,
I suspect Second Husband regretted introducing G to Old Lass
the very instant it happened. They get on like a house on fire, my
mother and G. It's not long before she disappears, blinded by the
embroidered stars on his hideous hippie pants, lost in an era that
died out, burnt to the ground long ago.

CHAPTER 11

I Fucking Hate Addicts

I have been related to addiction for as long as I can remember. When I am 14, Old Lass tells me of the night My Father tried crack for the first time, when I was six months along in her belly. I am self-indulgent and sincere in how hard I take the discovery of this piece of information. It isn't news to me that My Father is synonymous with drugs. It's not as though I've ever known any differently. A sober him. But I am less than an infant, I am a foetus, and I feel the full force of not being good enough.

I consider what type of man cares more for himself and a crack pipe than his wife with a growing belly, a baby, a toddler. People tell me – and continue to tell me for the rest of my life – that addiction is a disease.

And I know this, logically.

Yet, still I think: Fuck logic.

And: I fucking hate addicts.

Protector & Soul and I stage our first intervention when I am 11. Old Lass is barely there, in the house. Barely there, in her mind. A visitor, she slinks in every afternoon after hours spent smoking pot with G in his home. 'Having coffee,' she calls it. Every time I phone and ask her when she'll be back to spend time with us and with her one-year-old son, she is agitated and angry and hates that I call, and makes no effort to disguise her irritation. Eventually, I call in a rather feeble attempt to demand that she come home. I want to know when she'll be available to be a mother. Not to me – I'm grown enough. But I am a grown 11-year-old, I am not a grown parent. Still, I want to want to spend time with Stinky. I want to want to change his nappies because sometimes it's fun pretending to be an adult. Eventually she stops answering her phone when I call. I don't ever remember saving it, but I have always had G's number in my phone. And so I phone and sometimes he answers and sometimes he doesn't. Whenever he does, I am always polite. I am the polite, furious child playing the fool and I wonder whether he can pick up on my hatred for him. I wonder whether my venom seeps through the cracks and holes in the mouthpiece and flows through the wires and the air and swoops up his own line, through his own cracks. Whether it explodes in his big ear and screams and screams or, more terrifyingly, whether it whispers:

Hey, man, you and your dirty green grass, don't you see what you're doing? You and Old Lass call each other friends. So you know she has kids, one young enough to mutilate hideous antique paintings with thick skewered lines of a permanent marker. Don't you wonder who's at her home making lunch and scrubbing black ink off little thumbs and being a parent being a parent being a parent? Don't you care that you have stolen a mother and replaced her with a hollow woman who comes home stinking her stale breath at us before disappearing into a corner of the dusky garden? Don't you care that the thick wad of 'pot pencils' you give her, held together so snugly by an elastic band, will get her arrested on the road between the drive from your home to hers? Don't you care that while you're making money off of her weakness, she could be out making money of her own? She could have a job? She could be a grown-up? Don't you care that there are two young girls, a tiger and a mouse, who blame you for everything?

I don't think my venom reaches further than my own front door … How could it? How susceptible can a man who wears a trillion more colours than there are in a crayon box and is higher than Kilimanjaro actually be to the cries of a young girl who isn't even his own?

Everything's groovy, man.

He answers, and I ask him, pretending I am stupid, that I am the fool (and he believes me because I am a child), if my mom is with him.

Yes, he says.

I ask if he knows when she'll be home.

Soon, he says.

I thank him. I hang up.

I am polite every single time I make these calls because I have to be. I am polite because if I am rude he might stop answering the phone when he sees my name flashing on his screen. I am polite because now that Old Lass rejects my calls, this is the only way I can remind her she has children at home – via the looks of stoned irritation she and G likely exchange whenever it is me on the other end of his ear.

In the evenings, Parkhurst 2 fills with Second Husband's friends, who have now become Old Lass's friends. People flow through the white gate, crunch their way up the gravel path and make a beeline for the fridge. Beers are pulled out from within, their necks nicked on antique table tops, their metal lids slammed with hard palms, they're thrown back within, into the visitors. Everyone drinks and smokes and it is a Tuesday or a Thursday or a Sunday and everyone in this house does not want to fucking be here. They don't want to be anywhere, to exist anywhere.

Protector & Soul and I want so desperately to escape these people who are killing themselves trying to escape.

It is 2007. Stinky is three years old. It's a Tuesday or a Friday or a Saturday night, and at Parkhurst 2 there are people everywhere. Faithless blasts through the speakers in the lounge and Maxi Jazz rounds each corner in the house warning people that inaction will kill them, kill everyone. No one listens to him, but they sway and move and drink. Second Husband, when he dances next to the dining table, leans back with his eyes closed. His back is arched so that it looks as though there must be an invisible pole protruding from the ground beneath him, holding him up. His left hand holds a Heineken, his right hand raised, index finger pointing to the roof, and he bounces up and down. He is fucked up and he loves life and hates it and wants to escape it. There is a huge black man who speaks French and sings 'One guatemeillaaaaa' every time Meila waddles past. He thinks it is hilarious and so do I, but only because I like his accent and think he's gorgeous. There is a blonde woman who drinks whiskey or vodka or whatever she can find. There is the gay couple, Eugene and Nathan, who were present at Second Husband's bacon pasta proposal. They're never not at the house and they're only sober on arrival – and only for about seven minutes before inhaling forgetfulness.

I am tired of being around the faux grown-ups. It's only 7 pm and Stinky is wandering around the house on his fresh set of legs, walking everywhere because he can. No one sees him, really. I decide to retreat to my bedroom at the end of the hall, close the door, escape the house of escapism. But as I make my way past the bedroom that Old Lass and Second Husband share, I see Eugene hunched over my mother's dressing table. In his right hand he holds a little straw and is inhaling lines of cocaine off a book on the table. The lights are off in the room, but the open bedroom door welcomes the hallway glow to spill in and illuminate the scene.

Just then, I realise Stinky is standing behind me, so little he's almost managed to slip through my legs undetected and into the bedroom. I swoop him into my arms as quietly as I can and run to my room. Eugene doesn't notice us, anyway. He has his eyes on the prize. I take my cellphone out my pocket and call my cousin, Nic. While it is ringing, I feel the full force of the trouble this will get me into.

Nic answers and I tell him everything.

The next day, he shows up. He is like the big brother I've always wanted, but better, because he is my cousin and has therefore been raised by parents far saner than my own. As a child, I'd sneak into his purple bedroom when I was at my Nona's house and revel in the creativity that oozed from every wall of his room. He is a musician and artist and writer and I adore him because he makes it seem as though there is space in this world for exploration. It occurs to me when I am in his space that life is not only about necessity. It is not only about eating and sleeping and going to school and rubbing a sore belly and crying and trying to be a child. Life can also be about charcoal drawings of eagles and learning the guitar and wanting to tell stories and travel the world. I look at my big cousin and realise that there is room in this world for each of us, outside our families. The trick is to know how to insist that you take it up. To take up your space and to do whatever the fuck it is that you want to do.

I start writing stories for the first time when I am 11 years old. I have a sparkly purple notebook with a dark purple elastic that slings over the front to keep it sealed. I write stories about my best friends and school and boys and pigeons, and with each word I think of my cousin. I wonder if he'd be proud of me if he knew that I was trying to take up my own space by doing something I love. He is only 21 on the night of the cocaine call, but he is already fully grown, not medium rare, well done.

And when he shows up the next day, he confronts Old Lass. He calls Eugene and Nathan and threatens to ruin them if they bring drugs into our home again. He consoles me and Protector & Soul and tells us that he's always here for us. He doesn't ever say it flat out, but we know he is reminding us of how powerful we are.

Life won't always be like this – one day you can get the fuck outta here and do whatever it is you want to do.

CHAPTER 12

Have You Started Watching Porn Yet?

The last few years of primary school fly by. Sometimes I ache for them now. I am in a gang of five girls, and we call ourselves The Peanuts. God alone knows why, but the name sticks and continues to stick when we meet for dinners and wild whiskey dances and giggles every few months in our adulthood.

Growing up, these girls and I celebrate everything together. First periods, first bras, first kisses. One day in a moment of bravery at break time I ask them how often they masturbate. They look at me like I am fucking crazy and in this moment I realise I have two options: I can change the subject and we can all pretend I never said a thing, or I can own this thing; I can be honest about my honesty.

Ah, guys, man, it's not a big deal. Everyone does it and we shouldn't be embarrassed.

I celebrate this moment with these girls somewhat against their will – the first time I try to reclaim my sexuality. The first time I say the thing that no one wants to talk about, that thing that a girl should never mention. Perhaps I'm trying to find comfort in the collective. Surely everyone does this? I don't know how to put out feelers, how to gently broach the subject. How would that go? *So ... uhm ... do you guys ever, like, touch your fanny and feel good?* Too subtle. Too subtle for the girl who has never been veiled from the truths and horrors of sex. And so I dive the fuck in, vagina first. Once said, I feel embarrassed, relieved, powerful. I am now the one who shocks rather than the one being shocked. But am I doing to these girls what My Father does to me? This doesn't occur to me then, when I am 13 and in Grade 7. This occurs to me right now, when I am 24 and writing this. Am I honest and brave or am I trying to out-inappropriate everyone around me?

My Father returns from Greece two years before my Grade 7 year, fatter and with somewhat calmer eyes, back into my Yia Yia's house. Apparently, once his kind of sickness is gone, he's known as 'clean'. We don't go to his home any more, but he's adamant to still be a father so he does the things that dads do. Picks us up from school to drop us home at the blue house, takes us for lunch, asks about our day and tells us about his. He gets jobs managing restaurants and, just as quickly, he is fired. Each time he gets a new job, Protector & Soul and I bet how long this one will last. My usual guess is four months, and I'm never far off. He tells us how proud he is of himself for getting off crack, without rehab, without replacing the pipe with a deity, without one or two or 12 steps, only with his sheer force of will and some monks in the mountains on the other side of the world.

I'm clean, clean, clean. The next time I pick up a crack pipe, I'll shoot myself in the head.

Over the years, he tells us this again and again.

One day, he picks me and Tiki Hut up to drop us at a party. Tiki Hut is a tiny Portuguese Peanut with blue eyes, and she is funny and loud and we love each other because we have secrets in common. I never made her feel embarrassed the first time I went to her home and saw her father sitting with dead eyes on the couch, drinking beer from a plastic cup like he did every night until he passed out. She never told anyone at school about how my home was drenched in excess, too. We do everything together, our tanned shadows joined at the hip as I help her smuggle peas off her dinner plate and into a tissue on her lap at her mother's dinner table. She helps me improve my abysmal netball skills long after B-team practice has ended. At night, before sleep at either her home or mine, we whisper our shared wish for a 'normal' dad and talk like grown-ups about how dangerous alcohol and drugs are.

Not long after Tiki Hut and I climb into My Father's car, me in the front, best friend in the back, he turns his head to the left and asks us, 'So have you girls started watching porn yet? What kind is your best?'

She and I say nothing. Not in response to him in that moment, and never in any moments after that to each other. I've yet to find a friend other than my sister with whom I have this horror in common, and even Protector & Soul and I will wait for many years to pass before we can speak these words out loud to each other. I say nothing and I wish the cracked seat of the Corolla would swallow me whole, but then I realise I can't escape anyway – even if by magic – because Tiki Hut would then be left alone with My Father.

I am baffled by how filthy the world must be if this man who is my father is considered 'clean'. The one who asks me when I'm 13 when I'm going to start wearing G-strings; the one who won't stop staring at the DD boobs that have taken over my chest, burying my mole between curved mounds; the one who keeps telling me how sexy I am.

The next time I pick up a crack pipe, I'll shoot myself in the head.

Me at age 11,

at 12,

at 16,

at 18.

Pick it up. Pick it up. Pick it up.

A few weeks before I start high school, Protector & Soul is skilfully arguing her way through a debating meet with another school, and I'm her cheerleader seated in a fold-out chair. She speaks so beautifully. In these moments I am always so proud to be her sister.

Yes, girl, you fuckin' tell them, I think as I perch on the edge of my seat and count the minutes until I'll be wandering the same high-school halls as her. I wonder if she'll let me sit with her at break time. I wonder how I'll look in the grey skirt and white shirt and blue tie that will be compulsory for the next five years of my life. *Anything is better than the god-awful yellow-and-brown dresses I've been wearing for the last seven*, I remind myself. As my sister sits down to make way for the member of the opposing team taking the stand, I notice someone that is, in my mind, a full-grown man, standing to the left of the auditorium we're all crammed into. He has dark skin, dark eyes like mine, and even from so far away I can tell he has beautiful hands. When Protector & Soul and I return home that evening, I ask her if she knows the guy who had been standing near the front. She tells me that he's the older brother of Toot, one of her best friends.

'But he's in matric, Christ. Too old for you.'

I decide I don't care how old he is; I wanna kiss him. Considering that the Peanuts are all going their separate ways, I spend the December holiday hoping I'll make new friends, wondering whether I'll cope with a high-school workload, but mostly, I consider the matric man with the beautiful hands and the warm brown skin, known as Pash.

The first morning of Grade 8 arrives and Old Lass takes photos of me in my new uniform in front of the white gate that reminds me how much My Father has fucked up, while with every crunch the gravel beneath my black leather shoes reignites my hatred for Second Husband. I put the fuckers out of my head though – I have bigger fish to fry. New friends to make. A new boy whose eye I gotta catch.

Within weeks of starting at the new school, I have uncovered the following about Pash:

He has four sisters.

He is really good at Geography.

He plays the drums.

I like two bands that he really likes.

He is in all the school productions.

His mom is white and his dad is black.

He loves Jesus.

The Jesus thing scares me for a while, and I know we'll definitely never have this in common. So, instead, I work with what I do have – but only months after summoning up the courage. One day I get his number from Protector & Soul (Sissie, I *know* he's too old for me, just please relax!) and message him, asking if he knows of any drum teachers in the area.

I'm dying to learn.

(I was not dying to learn.)

I can teach you, if you want.

(Fuck, I'm good.)

Oh my word (can't say 'God'), *I didn't even think of that – that'd be awesome!*

I show up at his home for my first lesson a week later, and I am wearing an outfit that makes me feel very 'Baby' from *Dirty Dancing*. I, too, want love to come from lessons. Only when I'm much older, and have had my heart broken, do I realise that it works the other way around. Pash stands behind me and shows me how to hold the sticks and I am shaking with nerves unrelated to the massive instrument I'm seated behind. During one of our lessons, our second or fifth or sixth, my hair gets caught in his shirt button when he is leaning down behind me. I leave that day, fuming, for not having had the nerve to kiss him.

One day after a lesson Pash asks me if I'd like to meet him at an outdoor mall near his house on Saturday, just to hang out.

I hand him the R100 note for the lesson, and say, 'Yes.'

This is how it all unfolds. Slowly and gently over the next few weeks, as we walk around a skate park and eat Chinese food and order fudge. I start to relax my hand into his when he takes it in the moments we are alone. I begin to adore him. I become great friends with Toot, my sister's best friend and Pash's younger sister. I spend time with his huge and beautiful family. I go to the park with them and learn to play weird German ball games and I watch *Harry Potter* with them and try to fit an entire, peeled naartjie into my mouth as a means of initiation. I am 14 and I'd marry into this family if I could. They eat meals together and no one is ever not sober and they play board games and they laugh more than I knew was possible.

One Saturday, in a cinema, Pash is holding my hand and I can feel his eyes on me. Eventually, he leans in and asks if he can kiss me. I say, 'Yes.' We kiss and it is clumsy and terrible and perfect.

At some point, while I am falling fabulously into my first infatuation, My Father and I are having lunch. He asks me how my drum lessons are going. I tell him they're going well. He asks me if there's something going on between Pash and me, if we're more than just friends.

I don't care who you bring home as long as he's white. And if he's Greek, that's a bonus.

These words, My Father's words I heard so often as a child, swim through my head and I know I can't tell him the truth. I say nothing.

'You can be honest with me, Christymou. I won't be angry.'

He seems super sincere. I wonder if the Greek mountains have cleansed him of his racism as well as the crack. I still say nothing. He sees the look on my face, the wheels spinning behind my eyes, and he gently implores me to open up to him.

'Ja, I guess we're more than friends.'

Hello, angry eyes. It's been a while.

He takes me home, screaming at me all the way.

WHAT WILL THE GREEK COMMUNITY THINK?

This goes on for weeks. I try to reason with him, because I am young and stupid and believe I can reason with someone old and stupider.

Everything comes to a head one morning as My Father pulls his car into the drop-off parking lot in front of the school. Protector & Soul leaves the car before I do, and My Father asks me to stay behind. He tells me that I must pick between this Pash boy and him. Pash or him. I tell him I choose Pash. He cries and screams, high-school eyes dart nervously over to me sitting in the car and I die of embarrassment.

He is apparently broken over the fact that I would choose one coloured boy over his honour in 'the community'. I want to point out to him that he put his honour in a pipe and smoked it away long ago, but I don't. Rather, I tell him that this isn't even actually about Pash (I know he'll be moving to Cape Town the second he graduates – I know we have an expiration date).

'It's about the rest of my life,' I tell him.

My Father, doing what he does best, balls his hands into hard fists and begins smashing them against the dashboard of the car, threatening to kill the coloured boy and his black dad with each whack of the steering wheel.

Pash graduates, leaves for another city, I cry, I slowly begin talking to My Father again.

CHAPTER 13

Breakfast Bong Tequila Sunset

I am a teenager in high school and I am hideous, at least to me. I spend days actively avoiding mirrors because I can't stand the sight of myself; I devote days to picking at my skin, waxing everything that can be waxed, shaving my vagina and wondering whether every girl's looks like Lord Voldemort when bare. I am deeply nasty to Old Lass – I scream that she doesn't understand me. I wear too much eyeliner.

I save every cent I can for a plane ticket for a holiday in fucking Durban of all places. Alexia moved there with her mom when we were in Grade 4, and after losing touch for a few years, I visit her and nothing's changed; not her smell nor declarations of being pre-diabetic.

On a Saturday night in Durban, I am 13 and I meet three boys, all 14-year-olds, tanned, and each drunker than the next. I decide I love the darkest one the second I see him. He is Portuguese and has curly black hair; and the next day and the day after that and the day after that, Alexia and I wake up at 5:30 am so her mom can drop us at the beach on her way to work. The Durban boys wake at around seven and wander down to the beach one by one. They wear wetsuits and go bodyboarding. I ask them why they don't rather surf and they shout at me and they tell me that bodyboarding is cooler than surfing. I pretend to agree, although I truly don't. Only years later when I am comfortable enough with them to show my annoyance, I refer to the act as 'boogie boarding' just to really piss them off. One day Bum Bum, the skinniest of the boys, starts assembling a plastic-and-metal contraption. Amidst their laughter at my ignorance, I learn it's a hookah. I tell them that they really and truly should not be smoking this hubbly-bubbly shit.

Smoking is bad for you, guys.

A year later, on my next visit, I try it for the first time.

A few days after that a bong is pulled out from one of their backpacks. I know exactly what a bong is.

I try pot for the first time at around 8 am on a Tuesday or Thursday morning in Durban, and I love it. And I hate it. Everything is funny and delicious and there is an air bubble in my throat that I worry is trying to kill me for being mischievous. The boys tell me to chill out, that it'll pass. It does.

When I return home to the blue house in Joburg, I am no longer infuriated by the plastic cereal Tupperwares filled with weed in the kitchen cupboard. Now, when Old Lass tells me, 'It keeps it fresh,' I think, 'Fuck, yeah, it does,' rather than, 'Be a mom and keep some motherfuckin' Coco Pops fresh instead.'

Tiki Hut comes over one night when we're in Grade 9; we're trying desperately to keep our friendship alive. I have gone to a government high school that my parents still barely manage to afford, and she has a full swimming scholarship at one of Joburg's most pretentious private schools.

I am cool now, man. I've purchased my own hubbly bubbly and, as we sit on the floor in the garden cottage, I decide that Tiki Hut should give it a try. Instead of putting water in the bottom, I tilt the bottle of tequila I've stolen from Second Husband until gold comes pouring out and settles itself in the red, glass base of my new favourite toy. I puff and I puff. Tiki places the pipe to her lips and feigns interest in being a 'badass'. I drink and I drink what's left of the tequila. Tiki touches the bottle to her lips, barely tastes the gold on her tongue, and tells me that (a) we're too young to be drinking, and (b) she has swimming practice in the morning.

For the first time in my life I am wasted, and poor Tiki Hut bears witness as my ludicrous, drunken laughter screeches out into the garden summoning Old Lass to come check on us. When she walks into the cottage, I am lying back on the tiled floor, still giggling, the empty bottle of tequila next to my head. My mother kinda shouts at me, but mostly she apologises to Tiki for having such a ridiculous friend.

'Well, I'd rather you experiment here than somewhere else,' she tells me as she walks out. By 7:30 that night, I have thrown up everywhere and passed out in bed. Tiki spends the evening playing with Stinky, and in the morning Old Lass gives me two Panados and says she hopes Second Husband doesn't go looking for his tequila.

It really isn't long before I realise how much easier it is to light a cigarette than to assemble the perfect hubbly, so I continue saving my cents for plane tickets and begin stealing Camel Filters from Old Lass.

One day, I am feeling so guilty – and so cool – about my recently acquired addiction, that I knock on Protector & Soul's bedroom door. We have our own bedrooms now, Old Lass having finally convinced Second Husband that it's stupid to save so much space for children who never arrive. My sister uses her bedroom to study and drink her weight in BioPlus energy fluid, and I use mine as a canvas for ridiculous song lyrics sprawled in permanent marker.

'Christy, I'm studying, what do you want?'

This to me means 'come in' and so I do. I go in.

'I have to tell you something.'

'What?'

'But you can't tell mom.'

'I need to study – just tell me already.'

'I've started smoking cigarettes.'

'Stop that shit immediately or I'm telling Nona.'

I don't speak to Protector & Soul for days, furious about the mother of all threats she's hung like a noose around my neck, but then Old Lass comes to me.

'Christy-nu, I've noticed something strange.'

'What's that, Ma?'

'Cigarettes keep going missing from my boxes and I'm finding stompies hidden in little spots all around the garage.'

'Yes, it's me. I've started smoking.'

'Okay … just hide it better and don't tell your sister that I know.'

And this is how Old Lass and I begin to bond, hiding under a carport, exhaling our shame into the night air. Mine has humps on its back and hers is green.

With Camel Filters comes great weight loss, and lose and lose weight I do. Yet, my Double-Ds retain their fullness and perkiness; in fact, they continue to grow. Everyone side-eyes Old Lass's chest when they ask in disbelief where on earth I got my boobs from, and I don't know whether I should love the ornaments weighing heavily on my chest, or despise them. My instinct tells me to adore them – they're a part of me and I can appreciate how lovely they look and how grown-up they make me feel and how much fun I have when I place each one in the palm of a hand and bounce them up and down when I'm watching TV. On the other hand, men are creeping me out more and more, and shirts that were once favourites are steadily being tossed aside. I see how my friends are developing – just as I am, but with a less determined bosom. When I get ready with them before we go out to movies at the shopping mall (read: walk up and down and see and be seen by other people our age while never actually watching a movie), I hear father after father tell them to put on a longer skirt, or throw a jersey around their shoulders. These are dads at war with the puberty that has befallen their daughters. Though they try to monitor their daughters' bodies, they know they can't, actually. They know that the second their daughter is dropped off and they've driven away there's a miniskirt being resurrected from the bottom of a handbag. They watch in their rear-view mirrors as jerseys are yanked off defiantly.

My Father is still playing a game of being a dad being a dad, and often on Saturday nights such as these, he is the parent doing the dropping off. I get ready at home with Old Lass and on the nights that I know he'll be collecting me from the house and taking me to the mall, it is an entirely different experience than when I jump in the car with my mom. I overthink everything when I know he'll see me. I wear less make-up than usual, I wear jeans instead of a skirt and long-sleeved shirts with high necklines. No matter the season, I complete the look with the bulkiest jacket I can find.

Whenever he arrives and gets out the car to hug me hello, I am traumatised by the arrival of my boobs. They are strapped into bras and pushed down by shirts and layered in a coat but when he embraces me I still feel the need to pull my chest as far away from his as possible. I fucking hate it when he hugs me. I hate that I hide my flourishing body from a parent, not in an effort to prevent being reprimanded, but rather to prevent being sexualised. I have a growing body but my mind is still young enough that I don't have the words for this feeling yet. I can't place my disgust. I haven't yet let my thoughts linger on childhood bath times or the sickeningly intimate sleepovers I suffered through in my early years. Protector & Soul and I have never verbalised any of this to each other … yet. I hate it and I can smell his breath so close to my ear when he says, 'Hello, Lolo.' I don't know when Mouse died, but she has. And I don't know who this 'Lolo' is, but when I climb into his car I wish desperately that Tiger were with me. I wonder when exactly it was that my sister and I stopped doing everything together, where Tiger and Mouse have gone, and while I know it's normal for siblings to go their own way, I feel in my heart the way a bee looks when it's caught inside a house after the sun has set; feigning a sense of direction while searching for its natural compass.

As weight falls off me with each stolen cigarette smoked, I begin to love my new shape. My chubby, round face is the first thing to change, and I welcome the whisper of cheekbones with a manic glee. I stop asking Old Lass to make fillet and mushroom sauce for Sunday lunch. I stop asking for homemade spaghetti and meatballs for dinner. I start relying on the two bowls of weightlossesque cereal I eat each day to sustain me. And for a long time no one really notices, and I am glad for this. I don't want Protector & Soul and Old Lass to worry over my diminishing size; I just want to keep shrinking.

One day I am sitting at the dining table, and I can feel my sister's eyes on me, on each piece of penne on my plate. I stare at the pasta dripping with Parmesan-infused cream, and I understand now what people mean when they refer to food as the enemy. The only thing I hate more than the calories on my plate is the sister egging me on with her eyes to eat it. Irritable bowel syndrome is a shitty, shitty thing, but I rejoice, even now in my twenties, every time I shed weight effortlessly during a stress-induced flare-up. When I am 15, the flare-up of my sensitive tummy befriends my new relationship with food with dangerous ease. When I eat the 11 pieces of penne, I shit it away within minutes after leaving the table. A stress-induced flare-up is the perfect excuse to stop eating, and it's when I am stressed that I most want to be skinny. These things hold hands, they love me and fuck me together. During all of this, Protector & Soul is dedicating herself to her studies. She wants to be a doctor and she is going to be a doctor. She wakes each morning exhausted after long nights spent studying. She goes to school, where she excels in every subject. She spends her breaks talking and laughing with her friends. She goes to hockey or netball practice after the last bell of the day, and then returns home and begins studying once again. She is still my best friend and my everything, but now she is my tutor, too. She is patient when she tries to teach me maths. She is patient when I return home in frustrated tears with another failed test in hand. She's less patient when I tell her that I am dropping regular maths for the lesser version, Maths Literacy, but eventually she comes around to my way of thinking.

'I'll never need maths, sissie. I want to do something creative with my life,' I tell her. She looks at me as though I'm insane, but at some point it must have occurred to her that her little sister is probably not going to be a rocket scientist, so she inevitably and reluctantly gives me her support.

We have inseparable hearts, my sister and I, but we are beginning to bash heads more and more often. She is livid when she discovers I smoke weed. I tell her that I'm allowed to experiment and that I'm in complete control. She is heartbroken that I get so fucked up when I go out; I tell her that she's not the boss of me. She smells the Camels on me every day, and one day I am so defiant that I tell her Old Lass and I smoke together and hide it from her. I leave her alone, stranded with the anxieties surrounding excess that we used to share.

I am a goddamn nightmare at this age. The reality of how violently I felt and behaved only occurs to me now as I type this. Like a stranger you would have preferred not meeting, thinking about my teenage self leaves me with a sickening feeling in my belly. I don't sit right, with myself. I have a child within me that I wish I could hug, a teenager within me that I wish I could slap, and a young adult who is trying to be kind to all of these parts of herself. I feel fractured, I am hard on myself. I am waiting for life to become easier – I believe I am owed this. I believe I have been through enough trauma and chaos that the universe is now required to be kind to me. Even as I write this I am in many ways still a self-indulgent teenager. I'm still overcome by deep sadness and search out embrace from my nearest loved ones; oftentimes any one will do, but romantic partners are the favourite choice. I know, deeply and truly, how lucky I am and how little I am owed by anyone. I awake on a Monday and I am empowered; on a Tuesday, I am defiant; on a Friday, I am a black hole looking for a bottle of whiskey, a dance floor, a means of escape to devour whole.

I wonder if everyone looks at themselves through a shattered lens of selves. I wonder how any one person can consider herself whole. I wonder how the fuck people befriend themselves, love themselves, forgive themselves?

One morning I wake up to get ready for another day of Grade 10, and I bump into my sister in the hallway of the blue house.

'Hi,' I say.

'Don't talk to me until I can't see your ribs sticking out any more,' she says, flatly.

I tell her to fuck off under my breath when, really, I feel proud. I must look deathly good.

CHAPTER 14

Olive Oil

I fall in love with Olive Oil, my first real love, when I am 16. He and I have family in common. His aunt is one of my mother's best friends and we all grew up together. As children, we would gather in his aunt's beautiful garden and eat Greek and Italian food under the trees. On a Saturday night in 2011, I walk into a party at the house that is now less children-munching-on-watermelon-next-to-the-pool and more cheeky-teenagers-drinking-vodka-out-a-watermelon-that's-been-soaking-for-two-weeks. When I arrive with Protector & Soul and my new friend, Red Lori, I see four teenage boys on a makeshift stage. They are tuning their guitars and all have long hair and tight pants. The lead singer begins to croon in an out-of-place American, rock-'n-roll accent and I decide I have fallen in love – and I mean it. He is short and beautiful and from within the thick outlines of my eyeliner, I know that he is the only thing I'll want to look at for a very long time. I grab Protector & Soul and gesture wildly for her to look at him, to drink him in the way I am.

'Sissie, I want to kiss that boy.'

She points, her finger shooting out slightly from her hip, whipping out a gun of clarification, and asks, 'That one? Christy, that's Olive Oil – we grew up with him. Don't you recognise him?'

I don't. Only much later do I marry the memory of a young,

blond boy with thick glasses strapped around his head to the vision of the boy with curly black hair making eyes at me from the stage. When his band finishes their set, I do whatever it takes to be near to Olive Oil. I stealthily follow him to the front garden and pretend to talk to Red Lori. She instructs me to stand with my back to him, to play it cool, while she waits and watches until he takes a seat so I can ever-so-subtly sit down next to him.

'Go, go, go,' she whispers, and I cover the few metres to the chair next to him with a purpose and anxiety so desperate that my ears drown out the world with a vicious whooshing. I sit down, so close to him, while Red Lori stands opposite me making mundane conversation about anything and everything. Olive Oil knows I am next to him, and when the conversation he's having resolves itself, he turns to me and says hello.

Red Lori vanishes the second his attention turns to me and I can barely speak through my elation. I am so grateful, in this moment, to be wearing my tight blue jeans and cute white vest with the black buttons and atrocious brown 'sloots' (dear god, they were half sandals, half boots), which I love. He asks me my name, I ask him his. We discuss our apparently shared childhood and the fact that we don't remember each other at all. He tells me he's at varsity studying a BA (I swoon, not knowing what a BA is); I reluctantly tell him that I have just started Grade 11.

During all of this, his mom walks up to us, barely acknowledges me and asks Olive Oil if he's been smoking pot. He tells her, no, he hasn't. She says he mustn't. When she leaves, he turns his focus back to me and says, 'I was arrested for possession a while ago. I'm in and out of court all the time so I can't have any weed in my system.'

I should have run. Run to the watermelons hanging from trees and stolen sips, should have got up and danced with Protector & Soul and Red Lori. I should have run and eaten my weight in the pizza scattered around the place. I should have run away and considered how little I needed another high person in my life. I should have run. But I didn't.

I am 16 and a boy who plays the guitar has commented on my sloots.

'I dig your shoes.'

And he has asked me to dance.

'Sure.'

And he's given the correct response when I ask if he still smokes weed.

'No.'

I should have run, but instead I believe him and I let him kiss me on the dance floor.

The next weekend, I drag along my two favourite friends from school, Best and Mimika, to the Jolly. It's a sticky and cheap bar in Parkhurst and no bouncers have yet been hired to check for ID. I am wearing beautiful, soft green pants and a white top and I spend 10 minutes too many getting my hair to look just messy enough. I am shy and I cake base over the spots littering my face and I feel gorgeous – and like I am about to vomit. Olive Oil and I have been messaging on Facebook for a week and he's coming to meet me.

'To play pool.'

Actually, to dry hump determinedly on a couch in the cottage when I sneak him into the blue house much later that night.

And we do. We kiss and grind and kiss and grind and this is so new and special and correct for my body that when he puts his hand down my pants, when he slides it into my panties, I am so wet I wonder if I should be embarrassed. I have no idea if this is normal. Up until now, all I have known is the rigid and dry masturbation I've come to rely on almost nightly, and the handful of boys I've kissed and let touch me during the few months before this.

One of them had been the first to finger me, but it was fleeting and underwhelming and it occurred in a dark alley behind the very same bar that Olive Oil and I have just stumbled home from. Steven and I had kissed, sloppily, with my back pressed up against the cold, wet bricks at the bathrooms behind the bar. He put his hand up my dress, pulled away the cotton of my knickers, jabbed his finger into me slightly, and I groaned because that's what you're supposed to do, isn't it? I initiated this, and I feel I am in control. So when I decide I've had enough of this being fingered business, I push him away, straighten my panties, pull down my skirt, and return to the bar where I drink 10 shots of tequila.

I initiated this, and so when a few weeks later I hear that he's telling anyone who will listen that I gave him a blow job, I do not know how to be angry. I don't realise that I'm allowed to be.

The next boy I kiss, after Steven, is the first to go down on me. I am on a family holiday in Mozambique and he is a friend of Protector & Soul's boyfriend. He is 19 and fucking gorgeous, and mildly entertaining but only when I am severely shitfaced. In the mornings when we all wake up, we have a bong for breakfast prepared by Old Lass; we go to the beach and eat sandwiches, also prepared by Old Lass. We tan and we swim and we smoke more pot and we buy deliciously chilled Mozambican beers from men lugging cooler boxes around the beach. At night, Gavin and I kiss. We make out at the one bar in Ponta do Ouro and he pulls me in closely. I can feel his hard-on against me while we move on the dance floor and I feel embarrassed because we're in public, but then I consider that it seems as though Mozambique has its own rules about what people can do in public. Here, 16-year-olds are allowed to walk down sandy roads smoking joints and buy beers from locals and dry-hump boys named Gavin in a 'club' with a sea-sand floor. One night, after the bar and back at the resort we're staying at, the troops are all scattered. Protector & Soul and her boyfriend, Chino, have yet to come home. The friend I stupidly brought along with me on the holiday has sulked herself into a deep sleep (she wants to kiss Gavin, too, but can't because she has a boyfriend back home) in the room she and I are sharing. And so Gavin and I find an empty room and he is on top of me and we are kissing and moving together and I am completely naked. At one point, he has laid me down on my back and peeled my thighs apart so wide that I fear he can see up inside my vagina, into my soul, where all my deepest and darkest secrets live. I come to learn, on this very night, why people refer to this thing as 'eating out' and, Lord Jesus, I feel cheated. *This is nothing like in the movies*, I think. *Why is he making such loud noises? He sounds like an animal. I literally feel like I am being eate ... Oooh, eaten out. Now I get it.*

He's tired of eating now and is lying on top of me once again, staring at me. He is wearing thin, silk sleep shorts and nothing else. I can feel him straining his penis against the silk and he is so resentful of it, this blue, shiny fabric. I have told him I am a virgin and that I am not ready to have sex yet. I feel the head of his dick, helmeted in silk and smooth and wet with precum, trying to get into me without actually getting into me. The thin, sticky fabric is a barrier against full-blown penetration but I wonder if it is a barrier against pregnancy.

I'm 16 and I wrack my brain for the information I've learnt during high-school sex talks.

Does this count as sex? I told him I don't want to have sex.
Why are his shorts so wet?
Will I get pregnant from this?
How do I ask him to slow down?

And then he says, 'I may as well just take off my shorts and put it in, we're basically having sex already.'

And I say no and I get up and get dressed and go to the next room and climb into bed next to my asshole friend and I feel like I've done something wrong. I awake the next morning and he pulls me aside.

'I just want to say that it's okay you didn't want to have sex – you're still the most action I've gotten this holiday. So, thanks.'

Sure thing, I say. And I don't look him in the eye for the rest of the trip.

When it comes to me and my body, I don't know what's okay and what isn't, what's mine and what's the man's, the boy's, the property. All I know is that I must make sure that I am always neatly shaved, and that my top lip is always freshly waxed, because I must always be sexy. Sexy and feminine, like My Father always tells me to be.

None of this occurs to me, though, when I am kissing and touching and being touched by Olive Oil. With him, I can feel in my bones that I am doing absolutely nothing wrong, and neither is he. With him, I am being explored instead of colonised.

A few weeks into my first love, Olive Oil confesses to me that he is also a virgin. He seems so nervous to tell me, all the while my relief is bubbling up, seeping from my pores. I am so grateful and I grab his cheek and I kiss it and I am 16, in love, and constantly wet with anticipation.

Around this time, My Father and I go for dinner and he asks about my life. *School is fine. Best and Mimika are fine, but you're still pronouncing their names wrong. Protector & Soul is good; she's studying really hard.*

And then he says, 'Who is he?'

'Who's who?' I respond.

'Who's the new man in your life? I can see in your face that you've met someone.'

I feel betrayed by the potency of the emotion that has steadily been leaking from me since Olive Oil stepped into my life. In this moment, I think about the last conversation My Father and I had about a boy I fancied, and I decided that this is the perfect opportunity to conduct an experiment.

'He's a 20-year-old musician, he's covered in tattoos and has a lip ring, and he was recently arrested for possession of drugs. Oh, and he's half Greek.'

My Father claps his hands together in delight and asks, 'When can I meet him?'

CHAPTER 15

Declaration of Green Day

Two months after Old Lass discovers me attempting to sneak Olive Oil out of the house for the first time, he invites me on holiday with him. One of his aunts will be there, and so will two of his young cousins. Old Lass adores Olive Oil. She is comforted by the fact that she's watched him grow from a baby into a toddler into a near-man; she is comforted by knowing his mom and aunt and grandmother. She is elated that her bratty teenage daughter finally has something to smile about. She helps me pack my bag for the seaside trip.

A few weeks before we leave for the holiday house in Ballito, Olive Oil comes over to my house, rejoicing that his ordeal with the law has come to an end. He receives a slap on the wrist and community service. His name is cleared altogether. No more court dates, no more random drug testing. After sharing his news with me, he calls his best friend, Riz. On the other end of the line I hear a pack of musicians yelping with joy.

Olive Oil hangs up and announces, 'Riz has declared a green day. I'm going to go smoke pot with him and the guys. Wanna come?'

So off I go, with my new boyfriend, to watch him smoke pot and meet my even newer, new boyfriend.

In the days that follow the green day, Olive Oil is constantly high. After the holiday in Mozambique I have cut down on my pot smoking, when it accidentally cured me of my 'eating disorder' via the munchies. But Olive Oil is never not high and watching my first love disappear as quickly as I've found him breaks my heart.

But he's 19, and all 19-year-olds smoke pot, right? It's the normal and the smelly and the selfish thing to do, but everyone does it, and so I say nothing, and I find it so off-putting that I stop smoking weed altogether.

On the first night of the Ballito holiday, Olive Oil's aunt and nieces are in bed by 8:30 pm and I assume my new boyfriend and I will go have dinner and drinks and come home to the holiday house and make out and do everything but have sex. But we don't go out; rather, he sets up blankets on the lawn, and we lie under the stars and we smoke together. I smoke cigarettes, he smokes cigarettes and pot. I love how romantic this feels. Romantic and sexy as we fondle each other under the covers under the stars.

When we begin to feel the chill, we slide the blankets off the lawn and move inside onto the couch. Within minutes, Olive Oil begins fidgeting, and not in a cute I-can't-help-but-finger-you-whenever-I-get-the-chance kinda way. He sticks his hand down the side of the couch, comes up empty. He asks me to get up so he can explore the folds of the blanket. His panic grows and I ask him what he's looking for.

'The head of weed that I wrapped up in that slip.'

I know what he's talking about. I saw him carefully fold up the dried grass and little twigs and few seeds into a white till slip after he'd rolled a joint when we were sitting outside. I don't know where it is. I am 16 and stupid, so when he returns from the kitchen with a goddamn head light strapped around his forehead, I go out into the cold garden with him once again, get down on my hands and knees, and help him look for his precious slip. It takes me 10 minutes to give up, to declare the pot missing and return inside to the warmth and glow of the television screen. When, more than an hour and half later, Olive Oil hasn't joined me on the couch, my irritability is full-blown. I walk outside and find him, still on his hands and knees, headlight still blazing from his now-sweating brow, surrounded by candles that he's lit to further illuminate the dismal situation. Like Sherlock-fucking-Holmes, he tells me he's found the slip! He's found the slip but the weed has fallen out! In a seance to eternal highness, in the centre of a burning ring, I look at the boy that I once knew – the one I must now leave.

He is on his hands and knees, on the first night of our first holiday, searching individual strands of living grass for stray pieces of dead grass.

He is urgent like Old Lass was urgent when I discovered the 20 joints in her handbag and she snatched them away, scared I'd toss them out the car window.

He is urgent like My Father used to be when he'd shove me into the back seat of his car at 3 am, or when he'd shoo me from the lounge when I discovered him at night, assembling his drugs.

He is urgent and urgent, as urgent as his addiction insists he be.

And I shout at him and tell him that this isn't what I signed up for.

'I fell in love with the sober you, you asshole. And now I already love you but you're not the you I once knew … but now it's too late because I already fucking love the you I know you can be.'

I shout at him while he looks up at me from all fours, feigning stupidity, and I feel tempted to summon demons to take him away, suck him into the ground, spit out the extinguished candles of this black voodoo setting.

Rather, he follows me inside, tells me I'm being a drama queen, and I cry in rage.

'Don't tell me you don't have a fucking problem. Look at what you've just done.'

Look at what you'll continue to do for five years.

Look at what I'll let you continue to do to me for five years.

I replay in my mind the hours-long confessionals Olive Oil and I have shared before this moment. On the very first night he came home with me, once our lips had been sucked dry and his thigh had become raw from my body rubbing itself along it, there was nothing left to do other than devour all the information we could about each other. I couldn't believe how easily tales of my childhood spilled from my lips. Not everything, never everything, with Olive Oil. But enough that I let him into a place inside me that had until now been occupied only by Protector & Soul.

I explicitly tell him how much I hate drugs. I tell him how deeply my feelings of worthlessness run after 16 years of coming second to substance. I tell him about my trips to Hillbrow and how warped My Father's mind is, how volatile and violent he is. I tell him about all the drug-related abuse I have been through, leaving the sexual abuse buried somewhere far away in the back of my mind. And so when we fall asleep angrily next to each other on the first night of our holiday, I feel duped. As though I, foolishly, have fallen into a false sense of security, only to have all my nightmares play out in front of me once again, by someone I thought should know better.

I told him about my pain, so he should respect my pain, so he should avoid hurting me with my pain altogether.

Only now do I realise how cruel, in a sense, I was. To have expected someone to mould themselves around my rough edges. To have expected my confessions, which I handed to him of my own volition, to turn to sandpaper in his hands. To have expected him to use my sandpaper confessions to file himself into what I needed him to be, to fit where I fit. I don't realise this then, when I am 16 and in love for the first time; I don't realise this when I am 22 and am trying to hand another man, a second love, my pain. I realise this only when my third love arrives, accidentally, and teaches me that the key may be to find someone whose finger doesn't collide with your pressure points at all. But that's for later.

My heart is sore, but it is 16 years old, resilient and a citizen of denial, and so the holiday continues. It is made up of walks to the beach, pancakes at seaside cafés, and kissing. But at the end of each day, Olive Oil insists on smoking himself into oblivion and passing out by 9 pm each night. He's learnt his lesson though – he keeps his pot in a Tupperware, sealed up tight and unable to escape.

After the holiday I return to school. Most teenagers hate school, but I genuinely and truly *hate* it. I find myself unable to care about the things I am not passionate about – and I'm not even entirely sure what it is that I'm most passionate about yet. I love history; I treat these lessons as though they are a storytelling session. The teacher makes it incredibly easy to enjoy the 40 minutes we spend in her classroom each day. She is skinny with short blonde hair, she gives a sincere fuck about the subject, and she has no filter when it comes to communicating with her students. She speaks to us as though we are humans who too are dealing with hangovers and attempting to mend broken hearts. I have had a few of these teachers over the years, the ones who are human. And I decide that there are only two kinds of people who become high-school educators. There are the romantics who think they can actually improve the lives of their students. These are the ones who are elated one day, still clinging to their desire to inspire change, and deathly sombre the next, when they recognise the magnitude of the idiocy they're trying to sift through in their classrooms. And then there are the others – the ones who are still bullied little children on the inside, pissing their nastiness along the corridors to reclaim a power they've never felt they had, pissing to push their agenda.

These are the ones who tell young girls they're sluts based on the length of their skirt (Mev. Afrikaans). The ones who tell us we should respond, 'I'm not interested, Faggot' if a homosexual should approach us (Mr Life Orientation). The ones who say, 'I saw what you wore to your matric dance – you obviously have no problem with men seeing your boobs' (Mr PE). These are the cruel humans who are somehow allowed into a space where young adults should be safest. Where young women should be empowered, and young, toxic masculinity should be dismantled. I find the fluctuation of my mood every 40 minutes at school severely tiring. I don't know if I am here to learn because of or in spite of. I don't know when to speak up (I confront the teacher behind the 'faggot' comment), and when to keep quiet (I am in too much shock to respond to being sexualised by the PE teacher).

And so I am defensive and stubborn and kind only to the teachers whom I believe I have something to learn from. My favourite teacher of all is my English teacher. She is young and incredibly tall, and wears only dark clothes with long sleeves, regardless of the season. She is shy and walks as though she's still not quite used to her body despite having resided in it for twenty-something years. She wears a Lord of the Rings ring on a chain around her neck and one Friday, when Mimika and I ask her what she's doing the weekend, she tells us she's 'going to a death metal festival'. I imagine her head-banging and drinking beer and it throws me. I am used to her soft voice reading us poetry and her slender fingers collecting the journals she's instructed us to write in every week. She is utterly confusing and Mimika and I begin searching her, abandoning our readings of a Brontë sister each lesson to learn something new, to confuse ourselves even more. We leave her classroom each day speculating over her recently dyed hair and whether she's hiding scars under her sleeves or not.

One day the whiteboard she's writing on is heavy under the weight of her mind maps, and she reaches up to scrawl her tiny handwriting along the very top of the board. Her jersey strains itself with her fresh length before retreating up her wrist and revealing a glimpse of her forearm. It happens in an instant, and lasts only for an instant, but Mimika and I see it. Trails and wisps of tattoos that insinuate the full sleeve of ink we now assume crawls up her long arm. We feel triumphant. We speak of this and nothing else for the rest of the day.

In the years after my sparkly purple notebook had run out of space, I stopped writing altogether. I never missed it or gave it much thought, until I started writing again at the instruction of this teacher. Once I did, I felt a deep mourning for all the time I'd wasted, all the words I'd buried. And so once I rediscover it, this first and soon to be greatest love of my life, I sit in my Maths Literacy classes (numbers and I have never been friends) and I write the lessons away. I dedicate myself, my free minutes and my should-be-otherwise-occupied ones with writing. I write a lot about Olive Oil.

Despite seeing the addict in him, Olive Oil and I are still very much besotted with each other, but we argue at every opportunity.

Four months after meeting him, I decide I am ready to have sex. But it's not as simple as that. For as long as I can remember, Old Lass has said to me, 'The day you feel you're ready to have sex, come to me first so we can get you on the Pill.' So when, the morning after I have decided I am ready, Old Lass walks into the lounge where I am sitting on the couch eating Coco Pops, I say, 'Mama, I'd like to have sex with Olive Oil. Can we get me on the Pill?'

Old Lass looks at me, turns around, and walks right back out of the lounge without saying a word. Perhaps I should have cushioned the blow, made her a cup of coffee first and held up a lighter to her joint, softened her, but I am defiantly casual. I am ready to bang and this entire home is so casual. Drugs are casual and booze is casual and sex is a demon hiding beneath my cells but on the surface it is casual. I am at war with myself. The freedom to fuck up and be wild that I have in this home is battling my desire for structure, for health, for normality, for anything other than chaos and chaos and chaos.

The next day I go ahead and have the sex anyway. It is a Sunday afternoon and Olive Oil slides an orange condom onto himself. My white cotton curtains get carried away by the curious breeze that greets and retreats from my window. He asks me if I am ready. I say yes. He and the orange condom enter me, gently. Is a condom really flavoured if no one bothers to taste it? We try to move together, we take our time. Eventually we find it, that sweet spot, and our eyes widen together. Thrust and thrust and thrust and Olive Oil says, 'Baby, sex is the best!' before holding out his right palm for a high-five.

Olive Oil's band is gaining in popularity, although the shows I go to on the weekends are mostly attended by the band members' girlfriends, sisters and, sometimes, parents, who are instructed to sit at the back of the venue. The four bandmates are all students, and do a stellar job of attending lectures hungover after performing in some of Joburg's stickiest bars. On Wednesday nights, one such bar swarms with boys in torn jeans and girls in cropped tops, and I ache over the fact that I'm unable to go because there's school the next day.

After hours spent arguing, Old Lass and I begin to bargain. She tells me that I am allowed to go to Olive Oil's weeknight gigs as long as I attend school the next day. And so I go, careful to never let My Father find out. And I get absolutely wasted. I quickly assert myself as the drunkest girl at all the parties. I hunch myself over disgusting toilets, staining the knees of my jeans on crusty, piss-stained floors, I have a 'tactical' vomit, and I return to the bar and continue drinking. I dance wildly at the front of the stage and I molest Olive Oil with my unbelieving and unrelenting gaze as he sings and plays the guitar. I am in awe of him and his talent. I am 16 and I am dating the lead singer of a band and I ash my cigarettes on the heads of the 'groupies' who squeeze themselves in front of me and try to make eyes at my man. When I get home from nights such as these, after being dropped off by a miserable designated driver or a metered cab, I move noisily through the kitchen and I make sandwiches or pasta and I drink all Second Husband's Coca-Cola and I pass out, collapsing into the few hours of sleep I have before I start getting ready for school.

I have never been one to shower in the mornings, opting rather for a lazy bath in the evenings, so when I arrive at school one morning after a Wednesday-night gig, Best and Mimika tell me I stink of tequila before asking me how my night was. *I can't believe your mom lets you go to gigs on a weeknight. Did Olive Oil stay over after? It's so cool that your mom lets you two sleep in the same room.*

Some days, I push through the hangovers with bacon rolls from the tuck shop and green energy drinks that the Hospitality teacher, a bursting-with-love woman, buys for me while declaring that they are the best-kept secret to recovering after a night out. Other days, I am so exhausted that I insist my way into the sick room, where I pass out for an hour or two before slinking back into a classroom where I pretend to know what the hell is going on.

One Wednesday evening, I am standing in front of the stage at the bar like I always do, and my elated drunkenness turns on me in an instant. I am deeply sad, and my consciousness leaves my body and floats above it. I am in this place, filled to the brim with tequila, dreading school the next day, and I am out of this place, looking at a girl who should be at home in bed. My sadness turns to fury and I wonder why it is that Old Lass doesn't give more of a shit. I wonder why she doesn't refuse to let me make a habit of excess. I wonder why she doesn't insist that I be a child. Another wave of rage crashes through me, and this time it's aimed at my sister. She left me months ago to go on her gap year, and I'm punishing her in ways she recognises and in ways she doesn't.

CHAPTER 16

I'm Not Being Sex-Trafficked, I Swear

I am in Grade 10 when Old Lass finally convinces Protector & Soul to take a gap year after being accepted to university to study a Bachelor of Health Sciences – a gateway to the medical degree she still has her heart set on. 'You're going to be studying for the rest of your life. You should take a break while you have the chance.' And so my sister pours all the energy she's grown accustomed to spending on studying into waitressing, and she saves every cent until she has enough to leave. When she's accumulated enough, she is guilt stricken. The idea of spending her money on travelling instead of contributing to her studies makes her feel deeply selfish. Old Lass commences the convincing once again and, visa and money in hand, Protector & Soul flies to Cyprus where she takes on another waitressing job. She travels to Spain where she calls me from the airport, crying and apologising for never having taken my irritable bowel flare-ups seriously.

'There's a problem with my visa and they won't let me into the country. My stomach is swollen like yours gets, and I'm in too much pain to stand up straight. I'm sorry I never took you seriously, Christy.'

I thank her for the apology and when we hang up I smile because she is hurting. She's left me alone in this house with Old Lass and Second Husband and she's left me alone in this city with My Father, so I smile because she's hurting too. And then I continue ignoring her altogether. She messages me, spends a fortune calling me only to receive one-word answers, asks Old Lass how I am and what's new in my life. And with each attempt she makes to love me I move my soul further and further away from hers. My child-self is hysterical with grief. I have no idea how to function in a world that doesn't include her. I have lost my Tiger. I have no idea who I should hand my pain to. Each day I make the decision to be cruel, until the day I'm sitting in class and she messages me to tell me that many of our favourite bands are playing at a festival in London, where she's now staying with family friends. I am an asshole on pause, and I decide that, come hell or high water, I will go to London for this festival.

When I return home, I tell Old Lass my plan. She doesn't ask which artists are playing, but I keep telling her anyway, as though she'll perk up and understand my urgency if I say 'Skunk Anansie' often enough. She has no money. My Father has no money. When they remind me of this, I remind them that when Protector & Soul wanted to go on the high-school tour to Italy two years before, they didn't have money either but they made a plan. This clinches the deal. They tell me to get a job and save as much spending money as I can, and they'll cover the flights. A few weeks later, Old Lass tells me that one of Second Husband's friends has agreed to pay for half my flight if I take his money overseas under my name. Old Lass tells me that this is illegal but I don't hear her – in my mind, I'm already packing for the trip.

The day of departure arrives and I am vibrating with excitement. I have never been overseas before and, despite all attempts at cruelty, I am dying to see my sister. My Father drops me at the airport and instructs me, once I have checked in my luggage, to call Second Husband's friend to discuss our deal. He has a first-class ticket booked on the same flight I'll be on. I phone D-Bag – what I call Second Husband's friend – and he tells me to meet

him in one of the airport bars. I join him and another man at
a table and thank him profusely for what he's doing. He begins
staring brazenly at my 16-year-old tits and tells me not to worry
about it. Once his friend leaves the table, he tells me that should
anyone ask, I work for his company as a model. I have no fucking
idea what is going on. All I have been told is that I am 'taking his
money overseas under my name'. A few hours later, I take my seat
in Economy, read the love letter I have forced Olive Oil to write
me before I leave, and make small talk with an Irishman named
Ross seated next to me. I laugh in disbelief that the words he is
saying are actually considered English, and he cracks up every time
I say 'Ja' instead of 'Yes'. When the pilot comes on the speaker to
let us know we'll begin descending shortly, I decide to freshen up
in the cramped bathroom. As I stand up, Ross's cheeks go red and
he points to my bum. 'Did you have a little accident there?' I look
down, and caked to my ass is a block of chocolate that had fallen
between my thighs, rested beneath my butt and melted onto the
back of light grey leggings. I fall back into my seat where I explain
the chocolate debacle to my new Irish friend, and dig through
my hand luggage for the wet wipes Old Lass insisted I take with
me. Shaking with laughter, Ross, my human shield, walks closely
behind me down the aisle where I slam myself into the bathroom
and go to town wet-wiping my leggings. When I return to my
seat, the Irishman loses his composure once again when he inhales
deeply and says, 'You smell like a sticky baby.'

Once at Heathrow, D-Bag and I walk together to the security
gates. I hand a man my passport and the information slip I've been
handed during the flight. On it, I have been instructed to fill in the
address of where I will be staying during my trip. I have absolutely
no idea where our family friends live, and so when I see D-Bag
once we've landed, he instructs me to simply give the address of
the hotel he'll be staying at.

By the time I reach the Indian man with the kind but firm eyes at
the security desk, I am shaking. He asks me why I am in London.
I tell him I'm here to see my sister and my grandmother. He asks
me where I'm staying; my finger goes limp with anxiety as I point

to the hotel address I've written down. 'If you're visiting your grandmother, why are you staying at a hotel? How old are you?'

Luckily for the boys who have loved me and the men who have yet to, I am a fucking terrible liar under pressure. Unluckily for the boys who have loved me and the men who have yet to, I am fucking superb at it when I am composed.

This, however, is not one of those moments. I begin to stammer, and before I can stop myself, my half-truths begin pouring out from my thin lips. 'I'm 16 and I really am staying with family but I don't actually know the address, so I just wrote down the address of a hotel.'

As I say this, Kind Eyes is peering over my shoulder and staring at D-Bag who is waiting in the line behind me. 'Who is that man? I saw you walking and speaking with him.'

Vomit, vomit, vomiting up things that closely resemble the truth.

'That's my stepdad's best friend. He was on the same flight as me and he knows I'm nervous because it's my first time overseas, so he's just helping me with the process.'

The man turns his kind eyes into weapons of extraction. They zone in on mine, they narrow, and the next words that come out of his mouth are so quiet, his lips so still that when he speaks I half expect a god-awful ventriloquist puppet to emerge from beneath his desk.

'Are you being sex trafficked? If you are, blink twice and we will help you. You don't need to be scared.'

I have never had wider, drier eyes than I do now. Thunderbolts, lightning, hurricanes, nothing very-very frightening can force my eyelids down.

I lean in, staring him in the face and declare, 'I swear to god I'm not being trafficked.'

He considers my crazed expression, stamps my form and says, 'Okay, go on through.'

The timing of my trip is perfect. The day I land, Mimika and Best are packing their bags and preparing to go on a Prefects Camp arranged by the school. I count my blessings, hop on the tube to meet Protector & Soul at Paddington Station, and smile at a few Englishmen before realising that they seem frightened by my friendliness and that my South African quirks simply aren't gonna fly in this place.

Protector & Soul and I hug, we tear up, I force her to buy me a salmon bagel. I devour it and have yet to find a bagel as delicious in the years since that trip. My sister and I have more things in common now than we did the year before she left. We both drink – plenty. We're both willing to stand at the front of the stage that we know our favourite artists will be on for hours before they're scheduled to appear. We both know how to tell men to fuck off when they pinch our asses, how to chase our tequila swigs with sherry swigs to make all the swigs sweeter, how to laugh at tragedy until it becomes comedy, how to tweeze our moustaches and eyebrows in a dimly lit tent, how to be Greek South Africans in a place filled with pasty Englishmen. We're reminded on this trip how to be sisters. We begin meeting the versions of each other our distance has insisted we become.

For days, we dance wildly in the drizzle. We drink cider with our impeccable Italian friends, Daniela and Francesca. By the time Skin, the lead singer of Skunk Anansie, arrives on stage looking like a wild, gold animal, her movements harsh and inhumane and pure poetry in the way they jerk and flow, I have worked myself into a yelping mess. I cry when she starts to sing – I wonder how any one human can possess such power.

When it's time to leave, I discover my right chocolate-brown Converse high-top has been swallowed into the belly of the mushy, wet earth. I leave without it, and float back to South Africa.

CHAPTER 17

Disease? What Disease?

I return to the blue house – and to Olive Oil – feeling far more cultured than before. Like an excitable idiot, whenever someone asks me how my trip was, the first thing I think to say is, 'It was amazing! I can finally taste the difference between rooibos and Five Roses now. Turns out they're not the same thing.' And I mean it. Each swig of tea, instant coffee, cider. Each bite of pasta, chips, crumbed prawn. Each moment and taste I experienced overseas felt entirely new to me, despite the oldness, commonness, bore of each and every one of them. Even now, when I make the trip to Cape Town from Johannesburg, I can taste the difference in the air. It has nothing to do with the lingering salt or adamant wind, and everything to do with the fact that trips like these, to me, are spectacular gifts. I revel in the ability they give me to unbelong, even just for a moment. They force me to be less of the teenager I will grow up to resent. They compel me to be less the child of addicts, less the young woman shaped by sexual abuse, less the person who shares a city with parents, with demons.

Olive Oil and I continue being in love, fighting, exploring sex. He bonds with Old Lass the evenings in which they pass a joint back and forth. I bond with his mother, Mama Olive, while we paint our nails and pour over her bead collection and her drawers filled with arts-and-crafts materials. I am relieved by the context Mama Olive already has about my family. More specifically, about My Father and his drug use. I feel it takes pressure off me, in a way. Whether real or imagined, I find I am able to exhale, choke, cry in front of this woman. I adore her big Greek family. They laugh and eat and fight and eat as much as my own does – and then some more. They put enough lemon on each dish that emerges from the kitchen to satiate my Greek taste buds, and the fact that me and my bones share their culture with them makes it deliciously easy to slide right into the fold.

I am now officially committed to an addict, and everything feels brand new one moment, expired long past its sell-by date the next. I am repulsed by the taste of Olive Oil's tongue after he's smoked a joint. He tastes the way my mother's breath smells and I think of her when he leans in to kiss me, I think of My Father when I lean away. I think of Olive Oil, whether he or I like it or not, only in relation to everything I think I know.

But don't we all do this? As I wipe the side of my mouth after being cajoled into a smooch, I wonder if I can separate him from his actions.

This is something which, at this point, I'm trying to master with Old Lass. With her, I just manage to believe people when they say addiction is a disease. When she is so high that she is silent and still, unmoving, unmoved, like a seashell superglued to my fingertips, so beautiful, so stuck, so impossible to ignore and something I'm desperate to preserve, I remind myself it's a disease.

Disease.

Disease.

Disease.

But then I conjure up images:

of cancer patients,

of withering bodies.

I conjure up the image of a friend's perpetually dying father, of him in his wheelchair.

I try to reconcile these images of these kinds of diseases with the disease of addiction.

They fit poorly.

The result of a child at war with two puzzle pieces, each taken from a different box.

They're the same colour,

one an 'innie',

the other an 'outtie',

but they don't fucking fit.

Mental disease then? Perhaps.

I consider my friend who slices up her thighs when she is desperate to feel something. I am the only one who knows and we call it 'eating apples'.

I consider how she doesn't get out of bed for days at a time, most days in a month.

I consider the movies I've seen where women wander through white halls to white cells, muttering secrets of a universe reserved only for them.

This doesn't fit perfectly, either.

But it fits a little easier.

I am a smoker, so I know what it means to kill myself, 20 times a day, each time I light a cigarette. And I'm a selfish idiot, I know, but I am less of the addict that I despise because I'm still in my right mind even when the middle and index fingers of my right hand stink.

The cancer patient didn't choose cancer (unless, of course, they, like me, choose it 20 times a day).

My friend's father didn't choose to have his body betray him, locking away his lovely genius mind in his failing frame.

My other friend chooses to slice herself, but she doesn't choose each day for her brain and its chemicals to encourage her to do so.

But eventually, I suppose, the addict comes to rely on the damage they've done to themselves. I know my parents' cells scream to be remedied by the very thing that destroys them. I know logically that 'it's not their fault'. But I am tired of these addicts when I am six and when I am 16 and 23 because eventually my hands throw themselves up and my palms land heavily against my sides and my mind screams at their cells.

Something's gotta give – in me too, because it seems by being with Olive Oil I am choosing the very thing I swear I'd escape the second I was old enough.

One day, my favourite teacher, the English one, asks us to write an essay on absolutely anything, based on the topic of 'This is a man's life, we hold it in our hands.' I do this thing with men I love. But at this point I don't realise I'm doing it – it was the first time, you see. The thing I do is that I write the men I love letters. And in the letters I drop subtle clues and glaring bombs about what's going on in my heart. And I think that if it's written down, in words, how can they possibly ignore what me and my heart are saying?

These pleas have taken the form of love letters,

birthday cards,

inscriptions in books.

In those to Olive Oil, I beg him to be kinder to himself and to the world. His pessimism is fucking draining me, man. I know I can't be with someone who is all conspiracy theory and doom, while I, the eternal optimist, dedicate my days to finding joy in even a single raspberry. And so I ask Kahlil Gibran to do some heavy lifting for me.

During my second love, with The Italian, it is an inscription in a copy of *The Little Prince*, a quote about a rose, and it warns The Italian to love me well and to not lose sight of me, because we've been watering each other well, but lately I've been wilting from thirst.

For Milk, the third love, there is no quote. There is just me telling him, 'I'll be loving you always, from everywhere'. Also in a Khalil Gibran. Oops.

I don't know it then, with Olive Oil and The Italian, but these are prophecies. On the days I gave these men their books and my fears, I've woken up knowing exactly what it is that will destroy us. Each letter served, in my subconscious, as a bright orange warning cone:

We're fucking this up.

We're fucking this up.

I need you to not be so miserable and I need you to keep on watering me if we have a hope in hell of me continuing to love you as well as I do.

And I love fucking well. It's my weapon.

I realise one night, falling into sleep, that I love men so well because I want to ruin them for the next woman.

In the first instance of my manipulation via writing, I write my compulsory school essay on My Father, and on Olive Oil, and how I am scared Olive Oil will turn into My Father. It is impeccably dramatic, self-indulgent, and sincere. The last few lines are:

'We sat on my bed. With dented sheets and mountains for knees. And with a desert between us, I am two centimetres tall. And in the wake of my loss, and the glory of my chaos, I fell to my knees and prayed. "I don't want to end up with my father."'

CHAPTER 18

Things Even González Can't Fix

When I am 20, I am a waitress at a cocktail bar. One night, during a 14-hour shift, I drop a shot glass. It bounces off the floor and shatters into thick, tiny pieces. I am unaffected by my clumsiness as I flag down one of the cleaners to sweep up my mess before any shards sneak into an open sandal and slice up the feet of one of the many women I have plied with drink. Five minutes later, I feel the artificial silk of my black stockings wet and sticky against my left leg. I absentmindedly run my fingers over the wetness expecting to come up with fingertips streaked with muddy Jägermeister, but instead they are a bright red. I rub my leg with intention, bring up my hand, see more blood. A shard of glass, so tiny that four of them could have made up the head of a match, has embedded itself in the skin next to my knee. By the time I am sitting outside on the steps at the back of the bar, there is so much blood that my tights are welding themselves to my thin calf muscles. I discover that night that I was not built to see the insides of bodies on the outside of bodies. As I sit swaying on the steps trying to regain my composure, I rub the shard of glass between my fingers as though it is a genie's lamp. How can something so small result in something so big?

As I sit now, at my favourite Johannesburg coffee shop writing this four years later, I look at the tiny scar, two shades lighter than the skin around it, slightly raised, and I wonder how something so small could result in something so permanent.

I don't realise that, at 16, the essay about My Father and Olive Oil would have the same impact on me. It involves far less glass (none) and a lot more pain (a fucking tonne, actually). Never one to excel, when I see the small, impeccably neat writing of my English teacher curling itself into 90-something-per cent at the top of my page above my words, I am prouder than I've ever been. Here it is. My mind races ... A chance to tell Olive Oil how much I need him to stop being high, and here's the confirmation that it's written well enough that he'll have to listen.

'Can I read you the essay I wrote? The one I was telling you about?' I ask my curly-haired boyfriend with the muddled brain one evening as we sit on my bed. He sighs audibly, making no attempt at recovering himself, and says, 'Like ... only if it's actually good.' I don't read it to him; I cry in equal parts embarrassment and frustration instead.

Five years, a hundred evenings spent in front of a stage that he's played and sung and slipped on, and I never read the fucker another word of my writing since that night. It is easy though – it's not as though he ever asked me to. I barely managed to scrawl my inscription manipulations on the front pages of his gifted books. Barely. But I managed, of course.

Olive Oil and I fit together like a pair of socks. They must be worn inside out, though. To avoid being irritated, rubbed raw by the little seams of discomfort below the surface, I must adjust how I fit with him, how I look at our love, how I take on my role within our love. In the five years I spend with him, I stop trying to sandpaper him into a shape that fits with me. Rather, I turn to smoke and I float into the open spaces within him. Whatever he needs me to be, I try my best to be. He is potent and when he is happy he is the most joyous thing to witness. Like mine, his eyes wrinkle slightly around the edges when he smiles. When he is sad, which is often, I brace myself and sink with him into a dark place that is entirely foreign to me – and the place knows it. It tries its best to push me out. It is violent with me in bursts; it doesn't want me to lay roots in a place that isn't my home. And so I spend my time with my head in the clouds, the place called 'Christy Nu-Nu Land' that my mother and sister would joke about me visiting as a child, a whimsical place where my default setting is happiness, while my feet are held steadily in place by the sludge that Olive Oil's mind creates on a whim.

I wake and I am happy because the day hasn't presented me with anything to prove I should be otherwise. He wakes and he is sad because … the world.

In Grade 11, I am dubbed head chef at a hospitality evening we are hosting at the school. Armed with soggy pastries filled with over-spiced mushrooms, a main course so underwhelming I can't recall what it was, and dry malva pudding to truly drive home the message that no meals should ever be prepared in a kitchen 'cleaned' by high-school students, I peek my head around the door into the makeshift restaurant in an auditorium next to the Hospitality class. My classmates' loved ones are piling into the small room and taking their seats at the round tables. Eventually, I see Old Lass, Olive Oil, and Olive Oil's new roommate and old friend, Riz, sauntering into the room. They have slits for eyes, and their eyes are bloodshot. I sneak into the auditorium to greet them and, metres away from embrace, their smell assaults me and those around me with the force of The Hulk.

'How high are you all right now?' I ask my mom and boyfriend and boyfriend's friend.

They giggle. We're in a school and it seems apt that they're giggling like young fools. We're in my school and it alarms me that they are who they are in this moment.

'We have the munchies so everything will taste better.'

I get through the evening with my peers, and by the end of it we have all sweated everywhere and are covered in flour, dried mushroom cream caked into the beds of our nails. I make a quick speech in front of everyone in the auditorium to thank our teacher, thank our families for coming, thank-thank-thank. And, throughout, I have hot tears welling up behind my eyeballs. I am so embarrassed to be standing here and making this speech. I am not embarrassed by strangers witnessing the two Cheeches and a Chong who form my allocation of loved ones. I am embarrassed by the three highnesses witnessing me. How young and stupid and sober this after-school activity is. How stupidly seriously all the other families are taking it. Ooh-ing and aaah-ing over the disgusting meals they've paid a fortune to eat. How stupid my chef's hat. How stupid, that I'm head chef. How stupid the whole thing is, down to the very last mushroom.

When I leave for home with them, they tell me which dishes were gross and which weren't. They tell me I spoke beautifully. They discuss smoking more pot when we get back to the blue house. Throughout, sitting in the backseat next to Riz, I feel like a fucking nerd who has infiltrated the cool kids. Maybe I did their homework. Maybe I gave them a blow job. Maybe I was born through their vagina. Whatever it is, something gains me entry into their space. Whatever I choose not to smoke keeps me resolutely out.

Olive Oil and I break up, for the second or third time, not long after the Grade 11 hospitality event. One evening, as we sit drinking beer at the Jolly, he casually mentions that he may or may not eat some magic mushrooms the next weekend. To which I calmly respond, 'Cool. I may or may not break up with you next weekend.'

To be honest, I've never really understood why people despise ultimatums so much. I do understand that they can be a super effective tool for super controlling, manipulative people, but I don't think they're always that. Sometimes, I think, the fact that we know there are certain things we just can't bear presents itself as an ultimatum.

I can put aside my hatred of the pot you smoke. However, I can't deal with you accumulating another 'habit', because that'll push my hatred over the edge. So maybe I'll break up with you, maybe I won't. It is, whether we like it or not, a decision to be determined solely by your actions. And it isn't a warning or a threat, it's a calm truth.

'Okay,' Olive Oil says, more calmly than I've verbalised my not-an-ultimatum ultimatum. And so I fume. How casual our love is. That we should wait a week and see whether the weather agrees with a mushroom-fuelled trip. Let's wait and see what headspace Olive Oil wakes up in, how much he wants to escape from the world and our relationship seven sleeps from now. I fume and fume and tell him we shouldn't bother, we're over – with or without an extra dose of magic in our love.

I go home with Red Lori and I sob. The next day, a hungover Sunday, I lie on my bedroom floor and soak myself in sadness while I blast José González. I sob some more. Old Lass comes to check on me, asks me to talk to her, tell her what's wrong, and in this moment I don't trust her. I don't know how to gather the courage to say, 'You've given me a complex so big and green that I fear it's ruined me for teenage boys.' But I choose to see her, in this moment, as a mom and not as my mom. I tell her everything; I hand her my pain.

Days later, three or four of them perhaps, Olive Oil shows up outside my house and I am so happy that I only briefly check my reflection in the mirror before bouncing down the gravel path to accept his apology and thank him for choosing me over fungus. I have been staring out of the lounge window for days. I have eaten my cereal here. Brushed my just-washed hair here, chain-smoked my cigarettes here, staring out the window at the gate of the blue house. But when I get to the white gate, still standing after thousands of opens, closes, baseball bat whacks, he doesn't look elated, like I do. In fact, he looks more miserable than usual.

'Hi,' I say.

'Hey. Your mom asked me to get this for her. Tell her not to worry about paying me.' He holds out his hand in the air above where my palm reflexively outturns, and drops a plastic bankie filled with pot into it.

He gets into his black Ford and drives away.

I am overcome by a rage I must have inherited from My Father;

I am heartbroken with a depth I've only ever seen carved by my mother. When I find Old Lass walking down the hallway of the house, I slam the bankie into her delicate chest and wail.

What is this?

How could you do this to me?

I am unhinged. Everything, all the things that I chose not to say on the night of the restaurant evening, the nights, breath laden with pot, the morning's joints staring at me from a handbag on the drive to school, the feelings of lesser than, lesser than, lesser than that I have been trying to stifle, come spilling from me, and I am more sore than I ever knew I could be.

Are you in fucking cahoots with him?

Is one dealer not enough – you had to make one out of my boyfriend?

I can't believe you've done this.

Something in the face of Old Lass cracks, gives way. I see in her eyes that she sees in me how very much she's fucked up. I hear her apologise and it runs off me. I am surrounded by a film of oil and sadness. Everything slides off. Everything that is contained within me bursts. I slam my bedroom door and sob, loudly in the quiet. There are some things even José González can't fix.

CHAPTER 19

A Dealer Named Blacktooth ... Or Twelve of Them

My high school is made of blues and of greys. Of whites in long white socks. Blacks in long white socks who are supposedly at war with the Indians, in low white socks. Indians who sell me loose Courtleighs when I've forgotten my Camel Lights at home. Mimika, the only prefect in our merry little gang of three, stands guard outside the hospitality storeroom while Best and I steal sips and glugs of aged cooking sherry and colourful Grappa. One day we get especially tipsy, and then quickly fall into a somewhat accidental drunkenness. It's 10 am on a Tuesday and once we've spilled, laughing, into the corridor to get to our next lesson, Best moans when she realises she is Friday-night drunk and on her way to stand in front of a class and give a Geography presentation. I kiss myself on my mind's cheek for having dropped Geography for Art in Grade 10. I bid my best friends goodbye.

Mimika shouts at deer-eyed Grade 8s to tuck in their shirts while she shields Best from prying eyes and letting anyone close enough that they might smell her colourful breath. I walk to the art classroom where my crayons await. I can't draw or paint, you see. So crayons are my medium.

My art teacher is an odd and lovely man. Someone once told me he is a Jew for Jesus. I don't know for certain whether it's true, but I tell people that my art teacher is a Jew for Jesus. I know I'll want to write about him one day ... my gay (definitely) Jew for Jesus (maybe) art teacher who allows me to smoke cigarettes in his classroom during break time. He is quiet and intelligent and patient with the students who take Art solely as a means of sliding through the cracks. We sit in his classroom and while I burn my crayons, deep greens melting into purples into the blistering orange of a blob that is supposed to resemble a streetlight, I listen to him talk about a toilet seat sold for an obscene fortune, and tortured men and women born into an era that refuses to acknowledge their genius. I dissect abstract paintings and talk to my peers with just enough conviction that it almost makes sense that I am a part of this class. When I stumble into Art on the day of the Grappa, a slender friend whispers in my ear that I look drunk. When he's almost tipsy from his proximity to my pores, he steadies me under my elbow.

'Just sit down and be quiet and Mr Gay Jew for Jesus won't notice,' he tells me while he rolls his dark eyes playfully. I sit, and on Slender Friend's instruction, I am silent. Within minutes, Gay Jew for Jesus is approaching my desk, where I sit staring absentmindedly at the pigeon shit lining the bricks of the windowsill. I have four assignments and a thingy that I haven't handed in yet. He begins asking me where they are, before bringing his kind nose near to my face, inhaling, and shouting, '*Are you drunk?*'

Fearing I've finally pushed this lenient man over the edge, I begin stammering, scrambling for something to say. When I turn my heavy head up to respond, I see my friend has led the teacher away and is whispering something to him. A minute later, the educator is kneeling next to my desk. 'Just lay your head down and have a little rest. Sleep it off – no one has to know.'

Slender Friend sees my shock rising to meet my growing nausea, and once he's seated next to me he tells me in schoolgirl giggles, 'I told him you have problems at home and that he should give you a break.' He laughs at his quick thinking, and I laugh with him. *Genius*, I think. Then I lay my head down on the wooden desk shedding itself of blue paint and fall into a deep sleep.

There's nothing like a 'random' high-school drug test to wake teenagers the fuck up in the morning. No one ever knows who the first is to break the news, but once every two months or so, in the moments that tick away before the first bell of the day, students run down corridors, through quads, to far corners of fields and scream in a whisper, 'They're testing today.' It's quite beautiful, really. Groups that never interact with each other are suddenly telling the principal to fuck off in a shared whisper under their breath. The tests don't discriminate between races and sock length and cigarette brand. The random tests only care about the hues of your eyes, how disruptive you are in class or if, you know, you've randomly been found positive in one of the previous sessions. And so on a beautifully blue summer day, me and a few other souls find ourselves leaving our desks during homeroom and following Teacher Snitch down the halls and into an auditorium with toilets en suite to piss into cups. I smile at my peers who are less confident than I am, and they smile back at me. White teeth lined with black remnants of the charcoal pills they've swallowed en masse in a last-ditch attempt to hide the THC in their systems. A terrifyingly large teacher who, hands free, has been known to carry kittens on her bosom, instructs me to wee into a plastic cup. When she hands it to me in the bathroom, I thank her and I start closing the thin cubicle door. She grabs it, swings it open and tells me she has to watch me do it. 'I'm not hiding another cup of wee. You can search me if you like.' I am not even trying to talk back to her; I just genuinely don't understand what her concern is. I look down at my stiff, white polyester shirt and grey skirt and wonder where the hell she thinks I'm hiding any attempt at outsmarting the system.

'Just do it,' she says impatiently. And so I sit on the toilet, and so she stands with her back to me. After thirty seconds, the absence of the sound of urine hitting either plastic or porcelain is glaringly loud. 'What's wrong?' she snaps at me.

I tell her it appears I have stage fright. 'I genuinely have nothing to hide; I know I have no drugs in my system. This whole thing is just pretty weird.' Each time I try to engage with this woman on a human level, she becomes more impatient and irritable. She is convinced I am trying to play a trick on her. I am trying to wee. Minutes later, and still nothing. The queue outside the bathroom is growing – she has other girls she needs to make supremely uncomfortable. As she inhales to unleash more reprimand, we hear the gentle tinkle of wee hitting the bottom of the plastic cup I am holding between my thighs. I whip it out from between myself victoriously, and see that there is no more than a shot glass worth of piss in the cup. Warm tequila, fresh out the oven. She rolls her eyes at me, snatches the cracked plastic cup from me and sees my failed attempt at emptying my bladder as a personal attack, a final fuck-you. 'This should be enough.'

What feels like hours later, we are being called in, one by one, to a room where Mrs Kitten Tits and our school counsellor, Miss Mental, wait to tell us of our fate. When it is my turn, I climb the stairs up to the office where they're waiting, seated behind a desk.

'So, Christy, what do you think your results are?' Miss Mental asks me once I've sat down opposite them.

I look at her and am in disbelief that any school would have hired this woman to counsel anyone, let alone the 800 teenagers who make up this specific one. She wears floor-length cotton dresses that are so thin they expose the lines of her G-string, and it is so obvious that there is only a slim chance it's accidental. She flirts with the matric boys; she is nasty to the matric girls. Only weeks earlier, I'd seen her sitting on a desk, her legs perched on the chairs in front of her so wide apart that students had clearly seen a tampon string escaping the side of her knickers.

'They're negative.'

'Christy, what do you really think your results are?'

I want to say, 'Jesus Christ, this isn't an episode of *Law and Order* – get your heads out of your asses.'

But rather, I say, 'They're negative.'

'And what makes you so sure they're negative?'

'Well I hate drugs, so I don't do drugs. So there's that.'

They pause. They fucking stare at me. Their eyes are burning so viciously that no confiscated eye drops could relieve them.

Eventually, Miss Mental says, 'You're right. They're negative.'

More silence, more staring. And so I say, 'Yes, I know. I just told you that.'

The counsellor considers me for a few seconds before telling me why I'm really here. 'It's not so much the drugs we're worried about. It's actually to do with alcohol. We've had a few teachers complain about the fact that you come to school smelling like alcohol.'

When I tell this story to my sister and friends after the event, I tell it as a joke.

HAR HAR HAR. They had nothing on me, no proof I am always hungover.

What I don't tell my sister and my friends is that the second I hear my excess has been noticed, I begin to tear up. I begin to cry. I feel embarrassed and relieved and angry to be showing any emotion other than disdain to these women. But I can't help it. They are looking at me like I am a failed soul, and I feel like I am nothing. I mumble through my wet salt that I'll do better, and that I really do hate drugs, before picking up my schoolbag, slinging it over my shaking shoulders and making my way down the stairs and back to my lessons. I don't stop drinking, I just trade in a lazy evening bath for an urgent morning shower, and I continue recounting this story as a joke.

CHAPTER 20

Our Love is a Monkey's Wedding

I blink and, before I know it, I'm in matric. When break time comes, Mimika, Best and I melt into the lawn under a tree, the same tree, our tree, and begin the serious negotiations of lunchbox trades. I participate less in this activity in matric than I do in the first few years of high school. When I casually enter into a life of vegetarianism in my Grade 11 year, I sternly tell my friends that I can no longer trade half of my sandwich (Old Lass was, and still is, known for making a fuck-off delicious sandwich) for two Woolworths chicken samoosas. 'It just doesn't make sense any more. Start bringing veggie samoosas and then we can talk.'

With mouthfuls of food, we discuss the sex I am still exploring (do we ever really stop?). We discuss Best's boyfriend, whom I not-so-subtly despise. We discuss Mimika's boyfriend, who will later kiss another girl at our matric dance, which he attends as Mimika's date. We discuss masturbation like our lives depend on it – and, in a very real way, mine does. Perhaps not my life, but my sanity at least is restored in the early years of high school when I find two souls so similar to my own. Nothing is off limits, with these great loves of my life. We know each other intimately, and not in the charming way in which teenage girls kiss in the quiet of experimentation. Rather, in the horrendously gross and hilarious way that supreme honesty forces upon you.

One day at my home when Best and I are discussing our most favourite position (doggy style – duh!) I mention that sometimes I dread the thought of the very exposed view Olive Oil has of my asshole in these moments.

'I'm sure your asshole is lovely, babes,' Best tells me. And I concur because I despise self-deprecation and really, an asshole is an asshole is an asshole – how bad could any one be?

'Yes, I know, but I'm thinking I should start getting it waxed,' I tell her.

Best's eyes widen. 'Why the hell would you want to do that?'

I fish a cigarette out of my box, and when it is a centimetre from my lips, Best gently takes it from me, picks up my lighter, lights it, and inhales slightly before holding it out in front of me. I lean in, clutch it between my pursed lips and answer after a drag, 'Well because the rest of me is hairless, so why not my asshole, too?'

Five minutes later, Best has convinced me, after more negotiations than a thousand lunch boxes could have ever prompted, to look at her asshole. She has been bending over, knickers laying on the floor around her feet, spreading her pale, lovely ass cheeks apart and imploring me to, 'Look! Please just look quickly. I need to know if mine is hairy. I didn't realise this was a thing,' while I determinedly look away. Eventually I give in, turn my eyes on her, and groan loudly. The fucker's asshole is as smooth as, well ... a baby's asshole.

I remind myself I must be patient with my Greek self. What I lack in hairlessness I make up for in a year-round tan.

At my matric graduation, I am sitting in a hard black chair with a surnamed 'C' on either side of me. Alphabetically and one by one, we are all called up, handed a certificate and photographed shaking the hand of our fossil of a grade head teacher before he reads out a short statement about what each individual is planning on doing after school. When my time comes, the teacher – the one I've fought with months before after he's casually used the word 'faggot' during a Life Orientation class – begins reading my statement.

'Christy wants to continue to lunch with her girls. She is also planning on studying hospitality in the rainforest.'

I roll my eyes so hard that they fall from my head, roll to the tip of the stage and are caked in a layer of dust before flying back to their sockets where I blink wildly to clean and recover them.

What I'd actually written down was:

'Christy wants to continue to lunch with her girls. She'd also like to go volunteer in the rainforest in Peru [true] before returning to study hospitality [not true, but I didn't know what to say].'

After we've all had our mostly incorrect fortunes read, the prize giving begins. I turn in my seat and search out the face of Old Lass in the crowd of parents seated at the back of the hall. She looks miserable and bored, just like her daughter. My Father, seated at the opposite end of the hall from her, stands up, semi-evolved, and sneaks out of the hall through a side door on his bandy legs. I see his packet of Camels straining against his shirt pocket and I am envious and decide it's time to leave. I start planning my getaway strategy. I will leave, pretending I need to wee, through a door to my right, where I'll flag down Old Lass before we make a run for it. As I start to stand, my name is called from the stage. I barely register – I have my eye on other prizes. But the girl seated next to me pokes me in the ribs with her elbow and whispers, 'Christy, that's you. Go up … you've won something.'

I think she's joking, but when I glance around, everyone is looking at me.

Hurry the fuck up, will you. We all want to get out of here.

I walk up and onto the stage, all the while not knowing what the prize I'm receiving is for. I am handed a small trophy and glance down at the etching that crawls along it while I shake the hand of Mr Fossil whom I have no doubt is just as confused as I am.

'Someone-something-or-the-other Award for Excellence in Writing and Poetry,' it says.

My English teacher is beaming at me as I cross the stage. I am bewildered and, despite myself, very proud. Old Lass is hunched over her chair, half in, half out, clapping wildly because the five years in which I've begged her, halfway to school each day, to either turn the car back around and go home, or to 'just keep driving to Durban' are over. And because, after years of telling me as we'd sit, warming ourselves next to the fireplace and sharing a glass of sherry, that one day I'll be a writer, she sees I may one day believe it too.

My cloudy mother, my biggest supporter, always.

I don't go to Peru. I stay and laugh and cry with Olive Oil instead. I tend to put my heart first, so when I ask Olive Oil, months before graduating, if we can do long distance for two or three months while I travel and he casually says, 'Uhm ... nah,' I decide to stay. I choose him – again – and will continue to choose him for my first few years out of school, taking far too long to realise that it certainly isn't my heart I am choosing. I don't know this then, but I fear that he is the one-and-only boy who will ever date me, so I hold on tight until I've throttled myself spectacularly.

Throughout our relationship, Olive Oil's eyes are forever wandering, his fingers forever tapping away at messages that I read in the quiet of the night, long after he's passed out. Snooping is a terrible thing, I know, but when there are twenty-something-year-old tattoo artists or gorgeous, blonde drama students or models who live in Cape Town (where Olive Oil and his band frequently play and where girlfriends are definitely not allowed), you care less about the mischievous side of yourself that you don't like, let alone recognise. I put up with it for so long though that eventually I can't explain away this as a 'side' of myself to myself. Eventually I shake the hand and kiss the cheek of the girl I've become. One who sneaks, peeks, and is fabulously manipulative and smart when it comes time to explaining how I know my boyfriend is fucking around on me.

'Riz said something weird, so then I asked so-and-so and they said they spoke to *insert name of current girl I feel I am competing with for my own relationship* and so that's how I know something is going on.'

The first time a boy or a man you love falls to his knees, and wraps his arms around your own while begging for forgiveness, is a wonderful sight. How can you not believe someone who is in such a sorry state? I believe it and believe it, but each time it happens it is less endearing and more nauseating. If you ever want to make someone else's pain about your own, fall to your knees.

We continue, though. I continue to live in the blue house, although now I've moved my bed and belongings to the cottage in the garden where Protector & Soul has set herself up too. Second Husband has been fired from the job he secured after selling his antique shop years before. Now he is at home, and has traded in his beer for brandy, and I try every day to be patient with him, for Stinky's sake. Their hands may look nothing alike, but he is still my brother's father and I want so much for my little sibling to be happier living in this home than I am. Old Lass is never happy here. She doesn't have a car – it was stolen or sold at some point – so Second Husband gleefully watches as his wife begs to borrow his bakkie to go to the shops or visit a friend or go buy cigarettes from the garage up the road. I hate the bakkie. It is white and loud and its seats have buried the scent of ten years' worth of Second Husband's cologne. When we were children, whenever we would go as a family to an event or a braai or a god-awful Christmas party hosted by Second Husband's incredibly rich and incredibly horrible sister, he would sit in the bakkie outside the house, Stuyvesant dangling from dry lip, and press his hand into the hooter, unrelenting, for as long as it took for Old Lass, Protector & Soul and me to hurry to get Stinky ready and out the door. We were never late, and there was never any warning. One moment, Second Husband would be lying on the couch, all corduroy pants and bloodshot eyes, devouring the History Channel, and the next we'd hear the gravel crunching beneath his workman's boots before the car door slams, a metal amphitheatre for the hooting we knew is seconds away.

Many hours and 20 drinks later at whatever event we were at, Second Husband would just as abruptly declare it was time to go, to leave wherever we are to go back home. Each time Protector & Soul and I pull Old Lass to the side and tell her she has to drive.

125

She looks at her husband, slurring his way through the room with feet made of marble and she tells us to calm down. But we see in her eyes her agony over this. When we reach the bakkie, Old Lass and her husband are already four insults into their argument over who will drive. Old Lass never wins, so she climbs into the passenger seat and looks over the headrest at her children who crouch terrified in the back seat, and she tells us to calm down. She doesn't apologise for putting us in this position, because she feels it will make the entire thing more real. If she apologises for her husband being fucked, it means her husband is genuinely fucked. If she apologises for the fact that he is driving and we are in the car, then we'll realise the extent of how frightened we should be that he is driving and we are in the car.

I look at Old Lass often and I feel so many things. I bombard her with questions, all the time. Tell me about your first love again. What was Gran like when you were a child? What was Pappou like? How long did you live in Greece? Were you sad after you got your perm? Did you always want a nose job? How did you meet My Father? How did you feel on your wedding day? Where did you learn to cook so well? Why don't you like to bake? What's your favourite album of all time? What's the most important thing on your bucket list?

Questions and questions that take far too many years to actually start spilling from my lips. In one moment, I have always known my mom to be bigger than the label of 'mother'. She and My Father have left little room for illusion around the human condition. She is my mom and an addict and a gentle soul and a joy to everyone who meets her. She is witty – hilarious even – and when she thinks no one but me is listening, she is sassy and makes dirty jokes. She is limitless in her giving. She has a caramel core where others have peach pits. She feeds ... well, everyone. She cries easily and then stops herself, and then cries a little more when you remind her it's good to do so. She chooses horrendous men and hands them her heart. She then allows them to break it – consistently and for a long time. She infuriates me. She appears weak. But caramel hardens. She leaves, with nothing, to start afresh. She's done this twice. She is patient and adoring with every brand of human she meets: the doctor (shouldn't work so hard), the lunatic (knows the secrets of the universe), the opera singer (for them she will cry freely), the writer (may or may not be a lunatic but, too, knows the secrets of the universe), the alcoholic (they must have had a very hard life, be kind), the boyfriends who treat us like shit (Christy, has he eaten enough?).

I have never given Old Lass a gift that she didn't want to gift to someone else. She has never bought herself something that she didn't try to gift to her daughters.

'Keep it, Mama. You're allowed to have nice things.'

We talk about almost everything, me and Old Lass. We know how to glide over sore spots. They are ponds of brandy, covered in green muck. We never look directly at them. We look at the lavender growing in the garden. We fill phyllo pastry with spinach and cheese. We smoke cigarettes and drink double espressos in the car. She tells me to travel and explore; she tells me to stay and lay down the roots of a career I'll love. She tells me to do whatever the hell I want, that I am capable of doing whatever the hell I want. That I am brilliant and will excel in doing whatever I want. We sip sherry and I am in love with her heart.

We are in the back of a bakkie and Second Husband is swinging the car round and around a traffic circle on the road. Two wheels are lifted off the ground and I can see the road from the left window, closer than it should ever be. We squeal. When I am young I am thrilled. When I am old enough to know better I am terrified. Second Husband is drunk and knows nothing. Old Lass is high and sees everything and does nothing.

I pack my feelings for Old Lass into school lockers in my mind. Some are shut tight, heavy metal padlocks securing me from the kind of love that breeds anger. Others are open, adorned with pieces of pink paper and tinfoil balls, the remnants of superb sandwiches made from 6 am maternal love and irritation. To try to wrap my head around my mother is an impossible feat. Our love is a monkey's wedding. And who would want to ruin that by thinking?

CHAPTER 21

Hoot, Hoot

I am 18 with a full set of double-Ds, so I do the one thing I should never have done; I get a job at Hooters.

I rock up with my eye on the money, but quickly realise it's not what it's cracked up to be. And so I stay for the buffalo shrimp. I last only a few months in this place, all shiny wood, bright orange, shiny faces and dark tans.

My uniform insists on more than we've all seen on the surface. The rules are that I must never eat in front of the customers (they must see you as perfect, not human), and I must spend a fortune on beige bras and tan tights that stand in stark contrast to my Tripoli skin. I go out and buy the bras (the tights must be just the right shade of awful and are therefore purchased directly from the establishment). The girls are sweet and sour, depending on which of their regulars – old men whose weddings bands glisten next to beer fridges – are chatting with them. The bosses are all men.

Best and Mimika come for dinner one night while I'm working, and I feel uncomfortable. Olive Oil and Mama Oil come another night; I feel less uncomfortable. From one shift to the next, I don't know how I feel within this space. The girls are mean, the food is overpriced (but, admittedly, delicious) and I am forbidden to eat any brownies (there are simply too many calories in them). But I am not studying, Second Husband is not working, and there's only enough room in the house for one unemployed bum. TV remotes are joyous things only when they're not being fought over. And so I save my rands (two thousand of them), commit to a few shifts at a time and spend every cent of my tit money on a beautiful bamboo skateboard for Olive Oil's birthday. When he unwraps it, he is more elated than I've ever seen him. Had I known that wood and wheels could do this to a man, I would have built a cart – all planks and nails and rubber – from scratch long ago and pulled him along his life for the last two years.

I don't have a car and neither does Old Lass, so I am driven to my new job by My Father. He asks me each time he picks me up when he can see me in my 'outfit' and I feel weak with gratitude when I reply with the truth. 'We aren't allowed to wear our uniforms until we're on the premises. We have to change there.' I always feel sticky and icky when I'm in the car with him, regardless of what I am wearing, but now I am at war with myself, trying to keep myself safe. I lambaste myself. I feel that because I am sexualising myself I am no longer entitled to feel revolted when men do it – even if by 'men' I mean My Father. I remind myself that women should be able to wear and do and exist the way they want. I remind myself that my sexuality is mine for the taking, the resolving, the owning. But then an orange flash peeps at me between an unclosed zip and I feel less convinced of everything: of my place in this world and the origin of the discomfort I feel in this car. *Is it, was it, even that bad?*

Since my childhood, the location of my feet within My Father's car has felt like a precipice on which my sanity teeters. I must be careful to always keep them neatly next to each other on the car mat. When I would forget this, when I foolishly fold one leg over the other, My Father would take his left index finger, insert it down the side of my shoe, and stroke the arch of my foot. Out again, and in, and stroke, before my cells could recover themselves into ripping my foot away. And when this happens, when the hugs and the thighs and the nausea wash over me, I think of my sister and I reach out for her even when she isn't there.

For as long as I can remember, Protector & Soul and I have

always had certain rules that only the two of us knew existed. For example, when Our Father touches one of our thighs, the other, the one with the free flesh, must raise her voice to a shrill tone and engage with him about the weather, or this thing that happened in class, or the status of the lamb chops that sizzle on the braai. One must enthral him enough that he gets too distracted to notice as a thigh is removed from under his palm, so he doesn't notice the look of disgust and shock on the face of the body attached to the thigh.

For example, when I see a young girl sitting on her father's lap – God forbid he is bouncing his leg up and down – you must look me in the eye and ask me about my day while whispering between feigned words of interest, audible only to me, 'It's okay. It's normal.' I must never poke my sister in the ribs in an effort to give her a fright. She does not get frightened; she becomes terrified. I must, and she must, and we must be vigilant. Always. And so I am the tanned, eagle-eyed, Greek girl who searches out the truth of the rules my sister and I live by but have never discussed with each other. Like siblings who grow up under the eye of the same parent, we don't question our origin. We feel in our cells and bones our belonging to our surroundings, our shared DNA, our shared horror. But I am a perky 18-year-old with thick, beautiful hair and I am a master of carrying myself fully intact, out of one situation into the next. So when I climb out of the car to begin my shift, I think of my hair, of my boyfriend, and only briefly of the arch of my foot, which I carry with me wherever I go.

It's Valentine's Day. I have the evening off work, so Olive Oil comes over. We are on my bed in the cottage, moving together. There are lit candles perched on countertops around my room and the flames dance with Olive Oil as he moves up and down inside of me. His beautiful curls fall into my face and they smell like Mama Olive's shampoo and expensive nourishing hair oil. I want to reach out and stick my finger through a curl, my favourite curl, but we're engaged in the very serious business of having sex and a smell of something other than Pantene begins sneaking its way up my nostrils. I turn my head to the left and see that the white, stubby candle I'd lit and placed on top of my underwear drawer, right next to my bed, has been sexed from its sturdy position and fallen into the open drawer beneath. There, my beige bras catch alight and blaze, singing with the smell of polyester and inviting my other knickers to turn to flames. By the time I have escaped from under Olive Oil's body, a thick, slow smoke has gathered.

I douse the mess in water and hold out one of the bras in front of me, sex still fresh between my thighs but quickly retreating into reality. There is a black line dancing its way across the right cup of my work bra, slicing off the half that would hold and constrict the side of my boob. I decide that this must be a sign, but I ignore it. I open a few windows, climb back into bed and implore wetness in the face of burnt, beige horror.

The next day I arrive for my shift with stiff arms. I have tucked the corners of my tight, white, 'delightfully tacky yet unrefined' vest under the edges of my purple-and-black bra and have veiled my long black hair over my boobs. The manager takes one look at me and asks me what the hell I think I'm doing. In hindsight, a purple bra was not the smartest choice, but my options were limited.

'Listen, I'm really sorry. I did go out and buy beige bras but they actually caught alight last night.' There are old photos adorning the wooden panelling of this place. They show women in tiny orange shorts with big, eighties hair engaging in placard wars with women who are definitely not in orange and who are likely braless. All the world's women gathered behind frames to watch the curious case of the accidental bra-burning.

'Go home,' he tells me.

And I don't put up a fight. I fetch my bag from the back room, kiss my buffalo shrimp goodbye and I leave, knowing I won't be coming back.

It's around this time that I remember the money Pappou 2 left me before he died. Protector & Soul had received hers when she turned 18; and My Father had always told me that I'd get mine then too. When I ask him about it, he tells me we'll head to the bank the next day. I have forms to sign and things to stamp before the funds can be released. So off we go, bright and early, to sign and stamp and we're told to return the next day to get the cash.

It takes the smallest thing to set My Father off. I've always known this. But somehow whenever he explodes, it still takes me by surprise. I curse myself each time. *You should have been on alert. You should always be on alert.* So it shouldn't but it does shock me when My Father calls me that afternoon, his voice shaking in fury.

You are ungrateful.

You're a brat.

You don't deserve Pappou's money.

You're a child and you should be more like your sister.

You are selfish and a brat.

I listen to the words that lace together his insults and I realise it is me not having greeted him on the pavement outside the blue house a few hours before when he'd dropped off medication for Protector & Soul that has warranted this abuse.

I don't care about the money – and I mean it – but I feel my anger overtake my desire to defuse tension and I fight back.

We spent the entire morning together.

It had only been a few hours since I'd seen you.

I was busy with something.

You're trying to use this money to control me.

I tell him that if he refuses to give me my money, I'll cut him out of my life.

I sound like a brat, don't I?

I suppose that's what I was going for.

Pretend to be a brat, and spend R14 000 on finally having an excuse to cut My Father out of my life once and for all.

He tells me he's fine with that.

You're a brat and you don't deserve this money.

I hang up. And then I break.

My adult self is so relieved; I don't know why, but when it comes to My Father, it's always felt like something needed to *happen* before I could live my life without him in it. Something big and obvious and above the surface needed to occur, something that I can put plainly into words, because how else would I explain to people why we no longer have a relationship? The below-the-surface discomfort wouldn't suffice, because I'd leave it buried there for a while still. I couldn't blame it on his history with drugs, because then people would tell me to grow up and forgive him. *It's an illness, Christy. He got clean for you and your sister.* I want him nowhere near me, but until now haven't had the nerve or the reasoning, in my own mind, to make this happen.

My child self is so sore. I am tired of being called a brat and ungrateful because I don't believe these to be true. I spent my primary-school years attempting to woo classmates into being my friends with freshly baked cupcakes, and my high-school years loving a boy limitlessly and to my own detriment and my worst fear has always been being selfish. The word alone, 'selfish', cushions the feet of my soul with the carpet I used to stand on in My Father's house. I would stand tiny, pretending to be strong, pretending to be selfish, refusing to give him my pocket money from Old Lass because I knew in his hands it would warp into drugs. And a seven-year-old can't verbalise these things. I didn't know how to say, 'I'm trying to save you.' And so I let his words wash over me:

Selfish.

Pig.

Brat.

Ungrateful.

I know now that they are not true, but when I think back to the evenings I'd spend frosting cupcakes for other kids, cupcake currency, my young soul didn't know it all.

When I get off the phone with him, my mind is a mess. Old Lass and Protector & Soul hug me and scream into the air and declare My Father an asshole and we laugh and cry.

'We're going to the bank first thing tomorrow morning,' Old Lass says. I stop laughing and crying.

'Mom, I can't. He'll be so angry.'

'I don't fucking care. It's your money, not his. He can't do anything to us.'

I barely sleep that night. Old Lass and I arrive at the bank the next morning before the doors have even opened. When they do, we march in and wait at the counter of the man who'd helped me the day before.

'Hi, Christy! I'm sorry I couldn't help your dad yesterday afternoon. I told him you had to be here when we released the funds.'

'What do you mean? He came back a second time yesterday?' I ask.

The teller's face tightens. 'This is what I was afraid of. I had a feeling you didn't know. When I told him I wouldn't release the money to him, he started shouting. He's quite a scary man, your dad. Let's hurry this up in case he comes back.'

The bank door swings open and Old Lass and I already know, before his bandy legs have rounded the corner and his belly has begun bellowing, that he's here.

The bank is still quiet, but all eyes turn in their sockets and I wonder if, in this moment, I look as terrified as these strangers do. My Father screams. At Old Lass. He turns to me when it is my turn. He screams. The bank teller tries to calm him; he is then screamed at and threatened. Security is called. Even they look nervous. The teller taps wildly on his keyboard, and when he is done he whispers to me, 'Go now. It's done. Go.'

As he says this, I see My Father stride forward, raising his arms in Old Lass's direction and the security guards rush in. His anger makes him clumsy, and his round tummy makes him slow. A guard grabs my mom and me by the arms and guides us to the exit.

'I'll escort you to your car. Does he know where you're parked?'

'I don't think so,' I say.

'Hurry, before he finds you again.'

Old Lass drives like a cowboy at the best of times, and today, for the first time, I implore her to go even faster. I light us each a cigarette and we smoke together, our hands shaking, all the way home.

My mother locks us inside the blue house. We draw the curtains closed, and we don't emerge until late that afternoon when the engine we can hear running on the other side of the sky-blue boundary wall has revved back to life and screeched back up the road and away from where we are.

CHAPTER 22

Wicked Ice Tea

After wasting a few months slinking from room to room in the house, over gravel to the cottage and back again to the fridge, I decide it's time I find another job. Via a grapevine whose leaves are made of a musician boyfriend, a crusty punk friend, and a girlfriend of the crusty punk, I find myself sitting in front of two men for an interview at Joburg's busiest cocktail bar, in Greenside. They read my CV as I sit picking nervously at my nails and question me on my two previous stints as a waitress. Both brief, only one involving Spandex.

An hour and many questions later, they tell me I have the job and I start training the next night. As I waltz out of the place, I am elated. I have a new job at a place run by men who didn't once look down at my boobs. One of them, Brent, the owner, has stern, kind eyes. They pierce you only to make room within you for softening. The other, the manager, Pah-Lo, is loud and animated and reminds me of a younger, sober version of My Father – what I imagine he could have been if not for the crack.

The sticky shifts roll into each other. I begin at 3 pm, when I have to wipe away the lipstick imprints and tongue stains from the previous evening off the large, glass sliding doors at the front of shop. One colleague is 'cleaning' the coffee machine (don't ever order a cappuccino from a cocktail bar) while another takes a warm, soapy cloth to the tequila-and-vomit-splattered walls. We find just enough time to sneak in sushi or pizza before opening the doors at 4 pm and welcoming our tipsters inside. They ignore the greetings of the staff at the entrance and make a beeline for the table at which they'll obliterate themselves for the next how-many hours. One side of the place is lined with a white couch that snakes its way from front to back. The other by a wooden bar, high tables and high stools, all the better to accompany you on the way down after your thirteenth half-priced 'Wicked Ice Tea'. Bursts of bright yellow paint appear in the skirting of the walls, but otherwise the space is grey and wooden. In the hours when the sun is still up, its rays creep into the place to illuminate the green of the muddled basil dancing in tonic and spirits. They catch the eyes of the gummy bears soaking in liquor, fished out of long glasses with black straws – before they prove ineffective for sweet retrieval and are replaced with groping fingers.

The money pours in not long after I start, and I work hard for it. Leaning against the door of the storeroom, I inhale caprese tramezzinis splashed with Tabasco before re-emerging to decide which customers look suspicious enough to warrant a 10 per cent service charge. I make friends quickly. We are all, seems to me anyway, in the process of looking for our lives. Between degrees or cities or having fled a family home, we take up jobs as waiters while we wait for things to fall into place. We are all incredibly privileged and incredibly drunk most of the time.

For the three years I work at the cocktail bar, I feel as though I am waiting for my life to begin. Two years into the three, outside on the back steps of the shop, I tell Old Lass this while I devour a Camel before returning to my customers.

'I feel like I am waiting for my life to begin.'

So bizarre are the things that sadden my mother sometimes. Her eyes well with tears before her trembling lips part to say, 'Your life is happening right now, girl. Best you realise that.'

A heavy brass bell is hoisted into the air above the bar and chimes every morning at 1:40 am to signal last rounds. The staff rejoices and the customers groan and I prepare myself for my favourite and the saddest part of the shift. As the bell is rung, Pah-Lo fiddles expertly with the many light switches and gently illuminates the situation in the place, the hot air stinking of sweat and sweet perfume. Along the walls of the bar are huge, tilted mirrors eliminating any hope of privacy, and I look to them in the moment the lights change from blackout anonymity to the warm and sobering glow of sweet-jesus-where-am-I.

Women shoot up off the couches and tug furiously at their skirts while the men they were just dry-humping forget about them all together and yell and slur, 'Can I have a Heineken and a Jagermeiserrrrr?' The deep, drunken and usually regretted conversations in which near-strangers are enveloped evaporate as the Congelese bouncers walk in and bellow sweetly, 'You don't have to go home, but you can't stay here. Hey-hey-hey, it's time to go.'

Only hours later, after every customer has stumbled into the 24-hour pizzeria next door, after we've wiped down every surface and steamed every piece of cutlery, and only after we've done cash-up and counted our monies, do we gallop heavily from the place before crashing into sleep and preparing to do it all again the following day.

CHAPTER 23

Bank of Christy

The first time the blue house is broken into, I am having a
sleepover at Olive Oil's house and Protector & Soul is soundly
asleep in Chino's bedroom. Only two weeks before, we'd been
gifted jewellery that once belonged to our great grandmother. 'Fat
YiaYia', as she was known, had lived a long time, long enough to
plant delicate phlegm memories into the minds of my sister and
myself. An avid smoker for most of her life, she would sit in an
armchair at my gran's house and cough herself into a stupor before
yelling in Greek and lighting another cigarette. One day, years
before the Sunday on which I was born the wrong way round,
upside down, Pappou asks his mother-in-law, Fat YiaYia, if she
would like something to eat.

'Whaaaat?'

Louder.

'Would you like something to eat?'

'WHAT?'

Loudest and slowest.

'Would. You. Like. Something. To. Eat?'

'Ahhhh,' Fat YiaYia says, before curling her index finger
inwards and inviting Pappou closer. He leans in, and watches as
Fat YiaYia tugs on her left earlobe before stating in Greek, 'Too
much sex makes you deaf.'

And so stories travel, gain momentum, are regaled each and every Greek Easter, and keep people alive. Indeed, any time I mishear someone with perfect ears in my twenties, I remind them that too much sex makes you deaf.

When I arrive home from my sleepover, the double, wooden doors of the cottage are wide open. I think nothing of it. The washing machine is in the kitchenette and Nerrie, our honey-voiced domestic worker, has a set of keys. But when I walk in and start drinking in the mess I made of my bedroom the night before, it feels messier than I remember. My free-standing antique cupboards, distressed in blue paint a few shades darker than our house, have spilled their guts. Every item of clothing I own has abandoned its shelf and lies in a crumpled heap on the floor. My underwear drawers have been pulled from their shell and overturned. My burnt-orange duvet cover is covered in bursts of pink lace and red cotton and purple padding. It takes a moment for my eyes to adjust to my love of colour before I notice the box of Durex condoms that were in my desk drawer just the night before. The cardboard has been ripped to pieces and I see the three recently purchased condoms strewn around the bed. Two of them have been torn into, their lubricated muck oozing over the edge of a foil cliff. I recover myself, and notice the two emergency pregnancy tests I've hidden in the back of my cupboard ripped into too. This tips me over the edge.

Stinky's little eight-year-old face, dotted in beauty spots and freckles, enters my mind and I am furious. Only a few months earlier, I'd arrived home to find Stinky, one of his friends (my least favourite one), and Nerrie on the pavement outside the house. They were all doubled over and heaving, tears stream down their faces. When Nerrie had been able to recover herself, she told me that Stinky had been going through my things when a bottle of my perfume 'exploded'.

I'd run along the back of the house to the cottage, a spice gently piercing my eyes and sneaking its way down my throat. I pulled my vest up and over my mouth and nose, and when I glanced over my bedroom, I saw a bottle of pepper spray, designed to look like perfume, that I'd been given by a friend weeks before, lying on the terracotta tiles. The pepper spray particles had made their great escape into the air around the bottle, so I lowered my vest and began heaving, myself, with laughter.

That'll teach him, I'd thought as I made my way back to the white gate to check on Nerrie, the collateral damage, and to laugh at the two young boys who I'd finally defeated in the war of privacy.

But this invasion is on another level. I march into the house with the remnants of the pregnancy test box dangling from my hand, and when I find Old Lass I wave it in her face as though she should know what the hell is going on.

'Stinky went through my entire room! He trashed it!' I shout. Old Lass follows me down the kitchen steps, over the gravel and through the double doors, takes one look at my bedroom and says calmly, 'Your brother did not do this.' We can't agree to disagree, so I stomp into the lounge, turn off the TV Stinky is merrily devouring, and plant myself on the coffee table in front of him.

'Stinky, how many times have I told you not to go into my bedroom?'

My little brother immediately begins panicking and when he replies, mid-munch, Strawberry Pops sloppily flee from the side of his mouth, the spoon in his hand shaking. 'I didn't go in, I swear!'

I don't believe him, obviously, so I start yelling because I am 18 and an asshole and it seems like the obvious thing to do.

I rip the bowl from his sticky hands and tell him to 'come look at what he's done'. There, he peers tentatively into a mess I'm trying to convince him is of his own making. I look at his lovely, little face while he looks at the horrendous mess and I see his brown eyes widen. 'Christ [pronounced Christy, but without the 'y' – not in the Jesus-ey way], I didn't do this. You're very messy ... You sure you didn't do this and then forget that you'd done this?'

He's eight and he's smart enough to offer up alternate theories, but not smart enough to prevent me from spiralling even further. I am about to snap at him again when Old Lass calls me into Protector & Soul's bedroom. Her room is messy. Not messy like mine – never messy like mine, but far messier than her own mess.

Old Lass points at her window and I see a hole welcoming in the breeze where a glass pane should be. Neatly cut out of the wooden frame, the pane has been placed against the wall on the outside of the cottage and, until now, remains utterly unnoticed. We methodically start going through my sister's things and only when we discover YiaYia Dora's missing jewellery do we realise we've been burgled. Stinky is standing at the door of the room and when he hears this; he shrugs smugly, picks his bowl of cereal up off the counter I've slammed it onto and aeroplanes spoonfuls into his mouth as he makes his way over the gravel, up a few stairs, through the kitchen and back to the TV.

It takes a moment, but when it hits me, it hits hard. I sprint the few metres from my sister's room to my own, fall to my hands and knees in front of my cupboard, and see a big gift box sealed tight with thick, black tape, sitting calmly and alone in the corner of the cupboard. My sigh of relief is so elaborate that a noise I've never heard before escapes with it. There is a slit cut into the lid of the box, and beneath the lid is just over ten thousand rand. It's made up of tens, twenties, two-hundred-rand notes. I shake it and I hear the few five rand coins I'd slipped in through the crack thud from side to side. I am Greek, so I blame my preference for keeping my cash close to me on my heritage. After each shift for the last month, I sit happily on my bed, exhausted at 4 am, and count my tips before splitting the notes (and coins) into piles. One pile for shopping. Another for breakfast dates with Mimika and Best. A Jolly beer pile. But the biggest portion goes into my trusty gift box. My life's savings. I have no idea what I am saving for, but with each deposit I flip the box over and write lightly in pencil the date and amount inserted. That condom wrappers had been interrogated but my gift box bank remained undiscovered still baffles me, but I am grateful then and I am grateful now. Because even as I stood hugging the square box among my mess, I had no idea just yet how much I needed this money.

Over the following months, the blue house is broken into five more times. The brazen thieves hack at the locks of doors after crunching their way over the only security the house has: the gravel that warns our sleeping but alert ears to intruders. Second Husband acts slowly. After each break-in, he does no more than secure the freshly violated window or door from the outside world. Protector & Soul's door now boasts a white, sliding security gate. After the second break-in – through the dining-room doors of the main house – a gate is installed there too. Each and every morning I crawl, exhausted from my bed after a night of jerking upright and willing my ears to listen harder to every gentle noise of the night, to find Second Husband and politely ask him to secure my own cottage door. Each morning he refuses, until the morning I wake in that house and, bypassing him entirely, decide to plead my case to Old Lass.

'Mom, I just don't understand what the problem is. Can you please ask him to put a gate on my door?'

Second Husband bursts into the kitchen where Old Lass is about to attempt to placate me, and begins screaming.

I am a brat, a little pig, who shouldn't be in the house anyway. I should have started studying by now. I should have gone travelling. I should be anywhere than this house, and I am not welcome here. Little pig, ungrateful pig.

My mama screams back at him, and I scream back at him, but it's already done. Voice dripping in Heineken, seeping into the open parts of me, settling in, turned sour.

CHAPTER 24

My Neighbours, The Ravers

That afternoon I make my way to my shift at the cocktail bar and ask the day manager if she'll help me find a flat nearby; somewhere close enough that I can walk to work. With wide eyes lined in black and electric blonde hair, she tells me that the universe is smiling with me, upon me.

'I actually have a viewing scheduled for 11 pm tonight,' she tells me. 'The apartment is, like, 30 metres from here. You take the appointment, and if you like it, the apartment is yours.'

I get a friend to cover my tables and at 22:58, gallop down the street, black apron filled to the brim with lighters, bankies overflowing with cash and clean ashtrays slamming down into my thighs with each excited step. The studio apartment is buried behind a coffee shop that in a few months will have solidified my hatred for rich men in cycling shorts who judge me when I stumble home, half wasted and half hungover at 6 am on a Sunday while they sit sipping their 6 am espresso.

I greet the married couple, my soon-to-be landlords, and they apologise for the late hour. 'You'll see why we only show the place late on a Friday night now.'

I follow them down the clean, light grey halls of the block. Potted palms sit merrily in tall planters and in the middle of the building a water feature emerges from the ground, bamboo featuring as a backdrop. We get to a dusty glass door, and the number 1 stuck to it stares at me while Mrs Landlord jiggles a key in the lock, the wrong one, another, the right one. I walk in ... and I immediately know I want this place.

Having grown up in houses that resemble antique stores more than homes, I am refreshed by the clean lines, white spaces, marble countertops. I brush my fingers along each surface as I pass. I want to kneel and worship the porcelain of the toilet. I pull on a cupboard handle only to unleash a wooden drinks bar that silently unfolds from a wall, and I want to kiss the empty space where I know tequila bottles will soon balance. I spin around and declare rather than ask, 'I'm incredibly interested. R3500 all inclusive just as my friend said.'

Mr and Mrs Landlord glance at one another before nodding, and I can see the horror in their eyes at having to rent this place at such a low price.

Mrs Landlord purses her lips tight. 'And you're okay with the noise?'

The second she says this, my ears are swallowed whole by a thumping bass from behind the longest wall in the studio. I hear muffled, drunken voices making small talk laden with horniness, glasses being dropped, smashing; I can't hear it but I see clearly in my mind's eye the men in overalls sweeping up the shards. Indeed, right on the other side of my wall is the one-and-only club on the Greenside strip.

'We just need to be sure you're okay with the noise. We've had too many tenants move in only to move out a few months later because of it.'

'I'll take it,' I say, counting in my head how much the first month's rent, last month's rent and the deposit will set me back. *I'll have enough left over to buy crockery and cutlery,* I think as I shake my landlords' hands and skip back to my shift.

My dear Old Lass cries for days after I break the news.

'Mom, I told you I was moving out.'

'Yes, but I didn't think you'd actually do it.'

By day three she's come around, as she slumps her slender body heavily onto the cottage floor to assist in the serious business of bubble-wrapping up her daughter's life.

Packing up a life is a tiresome task. Packing up the life of a sentimental person is something else entirely. I screech at her to be more gentle with my odds and ends and she is patient and kind is more gentle than gentle can be.

The day of the move, Second Husband is only too happy to give up his bakkie for a few hours, so Old Lass and I lug my things into my new home and within hours it looks and feels like me. The whiteness of the studio quickly gives way to the burst of my colour. Red armchairs are draped in green blankets. A mustard rug is placed on the floor in front of the couch where I envisage the coffee table – to which I'll dedicate my next few shifts in order to afford – will live. My burnt-orange duvet cover is puffed up, piled high with throw cushions of blues and pale pinks. I adorn the space with all my favourite things and, when I am done, I thank my mom, give her a long hug, and walk the 30 metres to work.

Olive Oil doesn't help me move; in fact, he doesn't visit me in the studio until I've been living there long enough to make a mild mess of it. On the surface of my tanned skin, I pretend to find it strange, but deep within me I know he is jealous. After the first viewing I had snuck him into the bare apartment to show him around only to spend the five minutes we were there asking him if he was okay. His eyes lingered on the marble kitchen countertops, on the glistening shower and stone patio and the freshly tiled floors, and I imagine his mind wandered to the bars bursting with foamy beer and tipsy laughter lining the street that now made up my universe. And instead of being the supportive friend with whom I chose to share my excitement, I watched curiously as he stumbled on the wish that this were his home rather than mine.

I am resilient and thrilled, so I don't allow him to diminish my joy as I spend the first few nights in the studio eating toasted cheeses (my soul's remedy), and my afternoons making pasta (my soul's other remedy).

I have a rule, in this new home of mine. If I invite you in, I might as well give you your own key. So selective I am of whom I let into my space that the few loves of my life who wander in can be counted on my 10 fat knuckles. I never round a corner in this home fearing I might find my sink decorated with lines of coke. I don't have to sneak to the stereo to turn down the volume of early nineties rave music chewing at my brain. Every single Coca-Cola and yoghurt and beer and tub of ice cream in my fridge belongs to me (and the welcomed loves of my life who spend their evenings lazing on my couch). I spend three or four days a week pulling 14-hour shifts at the cocktail bar and my free time drinking in the others on the street. I am, for the most part, undeterred by the constant party on the other side of my wall. In fact, I am comforted by the cacophony on the evenings I fall asleep alone. The only indication that my home teeters on the tail of a beat is the glasses tinkering viciously on my shelf until the final-rounds bell has been rung and the DJ has deadened the music.

Maybe it is this emptier, more selective life that clears room for fresh mistakes, but, like a bad haircut, your forgetfulness insists you give it another go after each break-up, so I let My Father back into my life. Best and Mimika beg me not to.

'This time I'm in control. He knows I won't take his shit and I won't spend actual time with him. It will just make things easier for Protector & Soul.'

I write this now and I feel doubtful and I don't even know why it is that I truly let him back into my consciousness, but the words 'rather the devil you know than the devil you don't' raise their hands, bobbing desperately for attention in the crowd at the back of my mind.

I have spent a year avoiding entire suburbs, scared to run into him. I do not go to Rosebank Mall or the coffee shops nearby and if I am in a car that drives down the road where he lives I shrink into myself. I turn to jelly and flow down the seat. And I am tired of this. So I pretend to be strong, to eliminate the element of surprise. I give my sanity a bad haircut … and I regret it almost immediately.

147

One evening I arrive at a small theatre with Old Lass and Gran who's visiting from London to see a play directed by some witty Greek woman. As we are making our way in, my phone buzzes in my pocket.

It's a message from My Father. I hit the triangle on the video he has sent to me to see a woman's manicured index finger stroking her vagina. Up and down and up and down, zoomed in on the source of the universe and its pristine nail bed.

I panic and clutch my phone to my chest. What if someone has seen how disgusting this is? What if someone saw the message was sent by 'Dad'?

I am alone, I realise. Old Lass and Gran are ordering whiskey, so I force myself to watch the video. I need to understand why this is happening, why it has been happening, so I look to this vagina as the missing puzzle piece. Illuminate me, anything, please God. Up and down and up and down, before twitching open and revealing itself to be not a vagina, but a closed eye. The fleshy, hairless flaps of eyelids masquerading expertly as labia majora. I am shaking with revulsion when my feet carry me to Old Lass. I gently pull my mother away from hers.

'Look at what My Father just sent me.'

Triangle, tap, play. Where revulsion resided in me, Old Lass fills rather with fury.

She strings her curse words together manically, elegantly, and with each one I feel a sense of relief.

Cunt.

This isn't normal.

Fucking piece of shit.

I am not wrong for being so affected.

I begin typing my reply to the cunt-fucking piece of shit.

'This is so inappropriate. In what world do you think it is fine for a father to send his daughter this?'

'Lolo, have a sense of humour.'

'No. This isn't funny. It is not normal for a father to see this video and think, "Hmm, my daughter will love this. I'd better send it to her."'

He tells me a friend sent it to him and he thought I'd see the funny side and that he's sorry.

I should have ended it right there and then, should have burnt our entire relationship to the ground, but instead I walk into the theatre, take a whiskey from my Gran, hug my Nona hello and hope that the presence of these women, these great loves of my life, this beautiful council, just by being near me, can save my heart, which this evening feels six years old.

CHAPTER 25

The Italian

It is on the Greenside street, the one that serves as the place of my entire existence, where I first meet The Italian. Mimika and I sit at 2 am on a Saturday morning, riding the ass end of a Friday-night adventure, waiting for our pizza to arrive at the 24-hour joint next to the cocktail bar and whispering about the man at the next table. He is seated alongside a woman in a leopard-print dress and together they turn their heads to brazenly discuss me before leaning in closer, considering something, a thing, all the things, and craning their necks once again to gawk. After what feels like a lifetime – an uncomfortable lifetime – he hauls his big, thick body out of his chair and hovers over Mimika and me.

'Hi ... Can I buy you a pizza?'

'I can afford my own pizza,' I tell him while Mimika's giggles litter the seriousness I am trying my utmost to convey.

'I'm sure you can,' he says, his eyebrow cocked in amusement. 'But I'd like to buy you a pizza.'

'We've already ordered and paid for our pizza,' I explain again, my own lips betraying me and tugging upwards into a faint smile.

'In that case, can I have a slice of yours?'

Mimika's giggles flourish into a burst of laughter and she, my tipsy warrior, replies, 'Bro, she has a boyfriend.'

He bids us a disheartened goodbye, which I see in his cheeky eyes is feigned, before returning to Leopard Lady, whom I later learn is his sister.

Months of drinking, waitressing, drinking while waitressing and Olive Oil sex bleed into each other before I next lay eyes on The Italian. I am sweaty, flustered and dressed head to toe in black (which the owners insist I be), packing a tray with grubby martini glasses when he greets me and introduces himself. I wonder why he is so smug. There is a look on his face, one that seems to live there, that in one moment I want to slap off, and in another I'd like to brush my fingertips over, gently tasting the flesh of his temple. He appears more often than not on Friday and Saturday nights; we greet each other, I busy myself more than is necessary to avoid making small talk, I avoid looking him in the eye for the rest of the evening. Months more go by and one night at 6 pm, I realise I have been looking for his face in the crowd. As I count my rands at the 3 am cash-up, I realise I am disappointed that his small mouth and big nose and short black hair didn't arrive to greet me, hadn't arrived to greet me in more than a week. I wonder which bars he's been watering his insides at; which other waitress had ended a shift only to find a pizza and pack of cigarettes waiting for her in the kitchen, delivered by The Italian to the head chef at some point in the evening; which other waitress has wanted to smack and kiss his face. I feel a need to know where he is and why he's forgotten me.

This goes on for weeks. I carry my guilt home with me and tuck it into my bed where Olive Oil is already fast asleep (he'd long ago taken it upon himself to move into my home). One evening as I am hunched over wiping a liquor-soaked table with my filthy black cloth, my skin prickles and I know The Italian is looking at me. And so he is. He greets me and I look him in the eye, steadily, and I bathe in his small talk, greedily. That night I go home and I masturbate, laden with my familiar guilt and fresh fire, next to the sleeping Olive Oil while considering The Italian and his fingers.

I look at Olive Oil often, each year we've spent in each other's company its own lens. Sixteen is singed with the nutty tone of desperation. Seventeen is blue-and-white foam and wetness, and when I am 18, it is all of these things and more. Retreating waves of burnt, melted butter pasta in my heart. When I am in my twenties, we are beige, my love and I. But even this is set alight, accidentally, at times. Weeks' worth of a desert between us, between my thighs. Until an evening of dancing and touching pulls us lightly into one another again, where we meet, all white and blue and nutty and foam. And I love him, this love of mine, immensely. I love him when he goes up in flames in front of my eyes, when he is reduced to an ember of the person I initially knew; I adore him even when my fingertips are burnt trying to pull him in closer. Yet I keep thinking of The Italian.

In my fantasy, The Italian walks into the cocktail bar. The smugness is drained from his pores when I assertively place my hand in his, as I lace my fingers through his in the middle of the throbbing crowd and lead him to the parking lot at the back of the venue. There is a dark corner here, perfectly suited to the dark corner in the back of my mind where my fantasies flourish, and here and there I pull him into me, kiss him, drink him in, I let him sink his fingers into me. And this is enough, and foreign, and begins happening regularly in my mind when I dissolve into sweaty sleep. And I suspect guilt has an expiration date, because it rolls off my fingertips when I touch myself, sinks into the sheet on my bed, burns a hole through my mattress and disappears into the rocks of the earth, and eventually I forget it even existed in the first place. And where guilt once lived there is now a muted amazement, a thing I'd never say out loud – even to Mimika and Best.

I become acutely aware of how easy it is to live in my mind without letting my secrets spill out into my everyday life. I boil gnocchi and wash dishes and smoke cigarettes and I do all of these things sincerely with Olive Oil by my side, but I shake hands and make friends with the part of myself that he will never meet and who I've only just discovered, and it is the first time I have chosen to calmly climb down from the high horse my manic childhood insisted I climb up. Tiger in her childhood, Protector & Soul in her adulthood, had always insisted that things aren't always black and white, and I'd argued because the crisp air of my pedestal had made me dizzy with righteousness. But I learn she is right, and I know I will tell her that she is. I just won't tell her how I came to learn it.

I have been living in the studio for a few months on the Friday morning Old Lass is arrested. She is at G's house when the Hawks invade, all thick vests and big, black guns and at first she thinks someone is playing a prank on her, on all the people in the house. It is only when the men begin shouting for her to get out of the way that she realises what is really happening. It is only when they search her person, pulling the guts of her pockets inside out, spilling her handbag over and sending her insulin flying, that her panic blossoms. It is a miracle that in this moment she has no pot or cannabis oil on her. It makes it easier for her to choke out the words, 'I'm just here for coffee, I didn't do anything,' at the black boots that march by her. Nonetheless, she is put in a van and whisked off to the police station.

When Protector & Soul breaks the news to me, I am crippled with uselessness. I want to go see Old Lass at the police station where she's been locked up, but I can't. I want to phone her, but I can't; her phone lying in a police officer's drawer. I take the day off work, telling no one anything, walk from my studio in Greenside to the blue house in Parkhurst, and sit staring at the black of the TV while Stinky runs around the house. He's been told our mom has gone away on a spa weekend. I feed him cupcakes and when he asks me why I look so sad I feed him more cupcakes. I go home to Olive Oil and I cry, lambaste myself for doing such a useless thing, and so I drink some drinks and continue being blank. This goes on all weekend.

On the Monday morning I am told that Old Lass is being released, and I am weak with relief. I get another call an hour later and I am told, 'Oops, actually she's on a bus on her way to Sun City prison.' I am weak with fear. Only an hour later does this the messenger I'd like to shoot call me again to correct his correction. 'She really is being released, sorry about that.'

When my mom arrives home she is sunken, shrunken and aged. What little weight she had to spare has melted from her bones. Protector & Soul and I make her food while she showers. Second Husband marches through the house mumbling, 'Good,' and trying his best not to give a fuck about his wife. He does this so well that I realise he may not be trying at all. Livid and vindicated as he feels by his addict wife getting arrested for a habit he can't stand. He cracks open another Heineken and dissolves into the couch. Old Lass reappears dressed in white linen pants and a baggy off-white shirt. Everything hangs off her. She drips in fabric and guilt as she asks my sister and me to sit down at the wooden dining table that as a child I'd drip candle wax on to before peeling it way with an antique knife. I despised the mother-of-pearl handle that rested in my hand. My mind drifts to Sunday lunches where we were allowed to drink Coca-Cola instead of 'sky juice'; it drifts further along the aged wood to the memory of Protector & Soul's birthday the year before where one of Old Lass's friends had spilled an entire flute of Champagne onto her flourless Belgian chocolate cake. It wanders over the edge of the table, lands with a thud on the parquet floor, and from here I look up through the panels of the table and see all the interventions my sister and I have attempted to stage in this exact spot.

This one feels different for many reasons, the most glaring being that it is the first time Old Lass has initiated a conversation around her pot smoking. I am so broken by her, angry with her, filled with so much love for her, that when she apologises to us I am both her loving daughter and her worst nightmare.

I can't believe you put us all through that.

Please don't do it again.

We're so sick of this shit.

Have you checked your sugar?

You could be in jail right now.

I'll go get the diabetic bag.

6, perfect score.

Protector & Soul and I side eye each other when Old Lass tells us she'll stop smoking pot. Our eyeballs are deep pits of faithlessness.

Mine black, my sister's a lovely hazel.

'I will go for a urine test every month if that's what it takes for you two to forgive me and believe me.'

Black and hazel hope.

The next morning I wake up in my studio. Olive Oil is asleep, his thick curls falling over the space on his cheek that used to be my go-to for kissing. I try to stand up but my legs are broken after days spent bracing themselves for the worst. My throat begins tightening and my heart cracking, attacking its way out of my chest. I can't breathe and I wheeze for help and I crumple onto the tiles next to my bed and Olive Oil is awake now.

My irritable bowel greets my anxiety and they declare that they will be the best of friends. And so I spend the next year trying to shit away the panic and googling if twentysomethings can die of a heart attack.

There is a special little voice that lives in our cells. It tells us truths but because it whispers so gently, you could clear your throat and miss it altogether. On a still night long after my first panic attack, Olive Oil and I are on my couch watching a movie. My head is on his chest, body flowing along the cushions. He's sitting upright, in jeans. Only now do I realise that even then he seemed prepared to bolt at a signal I didn't know how to interpret. He's scrolling through his phone when I turn my head sideways and up to kiss him on his chin, and in this Monday moment the glasses in my cabinet are resting peacefully. The air slows and the universe is a stage for the voice in my cells.

Look at how he tilted his phone.

A car hooter blasts down the road.

Yes, consciousness, I know he barely moved. But you saw it. And you know – we know – something is wrong.

And something was. She was blonde and breathtaking and prompted an evening alone spent wrapping my thighs in cling wrap. Slim down, my body; slim down, my sadness. Hours later, I peel away my ridiculousness to reveal my sweat-splattered olive skin. A chorus of 'What's going on?' bleeds through my head and I begin to laugh.

And I say, *Heeeeey. Hey, yeaa, ye-ye yeaa-aah.*

Indeed, what the fuck is going on?

I pack leather jackets and cowboy boots and a boy's life into four black dustbin bags.

Come get your shit from my house.

And so he does.

And before you rejoice, ye loves who have been reduced to a clingwrapped ham of your former self only to find the strength to leave, don't.

A few weeks later, I take him back. But only after bumping into The Italian a week before at a party in town.

'I can see in your face that you're finally single. There's no excuse not to give me your number now.'

When he calls a few days later, I am elated. I jump and land heavily. I heave myself into the air and float. I stare at the screen and I don't answer and the phone stops ringing.

Only a few days after, I watch as Olive Oil falls to his knees, again. I fall for this sorry sight, again. And when The Italian calls me again, I let him ring into oblivion, again.

And I message him.

I'm sorry. I'm trying to sort things out with my boyfriend. But one day when my head is right and I am done with this foolishness, I will ask you out for a cup of coffee. And I'll apologise some more then.

It is then, I come to learn later, that The Italian deletes my number. And I think of him almost every day until the day I finally reach out to him, over a year later.

CHAPTER 26

Reunion of the Wendywood Girls

Old Lass has been pot free for a few months. In this time she has started her own catering business, and found the strength to leave Second Husband. When she tells me and Protector & Soul, we are tentatively thrilled. The blue house had gone up for sale before the arrest, and Old Lass's inability to wrap her head around setting up another home with a sad and angry man acts as a catalyst. Change one thing, change more things.

And this is how the three Wendywood girls end up back together again, in a brown-bricked home in Linden. We eat home-cooked meals and sit by the fireplace and stroke Meila and Jemima (the pavement-special delight that is our newest family member) and it is just as delicious and peaceful as the childhood home my mother created, except this time even better. Because now we have Stinky.

I begin studying Landscape Design and Horticulture at a small college buried in the middle of a nursery, and balance my job at the cocktail bar with the work I have begun doing for Old Lass. On weekdays I am covered in soil, and on the weekends I am splattered with either mischievous Merlot or Pappou's homemade chilli sauce that Old Lass has begun producing in bulk. I inhale the spicy air of our Linden home and I am happier than I have been in years. My improved temperament is muted only by the increasingly clingy boyfriend I have carried with me from home to home. A bizarre thing happens, I discover, after someone is unfaithful to you. They become alarmingly aware of the ease with which feelings can flourish with another person; how easy it is to tell half-truths and full-grown lies. And so they manifest in you what they've seen in themselves. On a Tuesday or a Thursday or a Friday night, Olive Oil wants to know where I am, who I'm with, what I'm doing.

And I tell him where I am and who I'm with and what I'm doing.

And he'll ask me again.

And I'll tell him.

I'm at that restaurant down the road.

I'm with Best and Mimika.

I'm eating spaghetti arrabiata.

And each time I state my truths plainly only to be asked to repeat myself.

I begin to fall steadily out of love, plainly.

So on the evening that Olive Oil asks me, plainly, 'Are you happy?'

I reply, simply, 'No. It's time we break up.'

Protector & Soul buys me a ticket to the New Year's festival she is heading to the next day, and I pack my booty shorts and pain neatly into a small bag. I am in the Drakensberg, surrounded by mountains, and I chug beers and flash my boobs and kiss a boy who should definitely not have been kissed, and I cry myself to sleep each night in the tent.

Two months and one new friend named Zen later, I am getting dressed for my first date with The Italian and I am ill with anticipation. I pull on a pair of green pants and a white shirt and some brown sandals and I remind myself how to breathe.

When he arrives in his blue car to fetch me, I stumble on a loose rock as I walk to him. He kisses me on the cheek and I can smell his sweat on him.

I consider, what kind of person doesn't shower before a first date?

Half an hour later we are sitting at the top of Northcliff hill.

I consider that a breeze must have come and lifted away his stench because I can't smell him any more.

Like a goddamn goose, it doesn't occur to me that my cells are falling chemically in love with his. I could have lifted up his thick, toned arm, inhaled deeply and declared sanctuary among the pitch-black Italian hairs.

Over Chinese food later in the day, I confess my wounds and truths to him plainly. I find I do this quickly in order to eradicate the men who can't handle me.

I tell him: I hate butterflies. People choke on them and die.

I order the flavour of my ice tea according to my mood: raspberry as comfort.

If I had my way, I'd sustain myself only on pasta and sandwiches.

I hate drugs. I hate people who do drugs. I hate conversations with people whose bodies and minds are hostage to drugs.

If I see a white, speckled-with-gunk under-nose, I will run for the hills, Italian.

'I used to do that shit, but I don't any more,' he tells me as I fold up the fortune of my cookie and slide it, a sentimental secret, into the pocket of my pants.

On our second date, I am wearing a backless leotard. We're perched on stools at a bar and, after ordering a round of whiskey called Hell's Fire, The Italian leans back and runs his fingers along the skin of my spine. I despise my Hell's Fire and my fish tacos because I want desperately for my mouth to be occupied with other things. I adore them because they give my thumping heart something else to focus on.

When we arrive at The Italian's house a few hours later to watch a movie, it takes about 11 minutes for the façade to fall away. We kiss and I consider the taste of his tongue. So different to Olive Oil's, so similar to what I'd imagined in the dark-corner fantasy I've dipped myself into over the years. He sits up and pulls me on top of him on the couch and with his teeth he releases the left strap of my leotard from my shoulder, the right following the invitation of its own accord. My boobs fall freely and rejoice in the groan that escapes from the back of The Italian's throat. He carries me to his bedroom, a leaf on fire. And we kiss and grind and kiss and grind and I place my hand on his chest above me, the full weight of his strong body pinning me to the bed. Tap-tap, my palm. So gently. And he flies off me, landing at the foot of the bed.

'I'll wait a year to have sex with you if that's how long it takes. I mean, I'd prefer we didn't wait that long, but I would ...'

He drives me home in his blue car and when I climb into my bed that night, I curse the period that had befallen me the day before.

All right, I think. *Let's let him think I want to take it slowly.*

My new boyfriend visits me at work. He tucks and pulls me tight into harnesses and teaches me how to rock climb. He takes me to the charity he volunteers at every Friday evening and introduces me to his young friends. He comes to my home and drinks tea with me. He strokes Jemima and makes conversation with Old Lass. Sometimes he brings raw steaks with him. And, shirtless, he fries them in our kitchen. This is how Protector & Soul first meets him. Frying up a steak real nice in the house of his vegetarian girlfriend. When he leaves, my sister comments on how brazen he is, and that he's old.

'He's only 30,' I say. But in the front of my mind I know how very strange it is to have my 30-year-old Italian coming round to the home I share with my family. And so he and I spend most of our time at his place, and we begin exploring our sex on his bed, and it is nothing like what I am used to. He is gentle only in bursts, in and out of the bedroom. He is determined and severe and his neck holds his head upright, at all times. The smugness that stumped me years before has not dissipated one bit, even once we've settled into each other's company. He is always cheeky and he always plays coy and when we have sex he does not look me in the eye. Not even once. But it is wild and new and I find myself slipping between the bed and headboard so often, legs flailing, until he has retrieved me from the space he's fucked me into that I don't have time to notice his eyes, or my eyes.

When his alarm goes off in the morning, he hops from his side of the bed in an instant, and I peel open my eyes and wonder if he has noticed the invisible line that is drawn down the middle of his king-sized mattress. We don't cuddle after our sex. I don't find him, during the heavy night-time, and he doesn't find me. And our bodies never melt wordlessly into each other. Before I have a chance to process this, to consider if I've helped in holding out the imaginary ruler while he drew a crisp, neat line along his grey linen, or if this line existed long before me, he has returned from his bathroom, freshly showered. He turns on Milky Chance, his speakers as loud as 7 am decency allows, and dances over his wooden floors. He is endearing as he glances at me while pulling up his Armani jocks, and I smile deeply and from my stomach. He is captivating when he swings his arms from side to side, clicking his fingers and shuffling his feet and trying to recreate fond boy-band memories but rather dragging visions of *The Fresh Prince of Bel-Air* to the forefront of my mind. He is dressed now, and a seriousness returns with each shirt button secured, but his playfulness continues to dance in his eyes as he makes me coffee. Mine bitter with some milk. His buttery and black and honey-sweet. We chase it with a thick, green drink made of the bottom of the sea and he tries to force feed me a banana.

'I don't eat first thing in the morning because of my IBS – you know this.'

Still, sometimes I peel back the rubbery green-yellow and I sink my teeth into the soft flesh and I stare at him and I want to make him happy.

The Italian and I spend our Tuesdays taking salsa lessons in Parkhurst in a garage-turned-dance-studio, and after, we eat Thai food or Indian food or sushi. One evening, we meet his friends at a restaurant on the same street where I was first fingered by Steven, on the street where I first met Olive Oil on purpose. I know most of these people, so when they cheer for The Italian and me to show them what we're learning in our salsa classes, I giggle nervously but agree. He twirls me into the cake fridge. It is a terrible mess of an effort and I usually wouldn't care about playing the fool, but there is a petite blonde at the table whom I've never met before. And she is a grown-up and a writer and the features editor at *Cosmopolitan* and I am a 22-year-old waitress desperate to be anything other than myself in this moment. I want to be a grown-up writer too. I say barely 10 words to her all evening. I barely look at this petite, scary beauty, Kim.

On the nights I know I'll be going to The Italian after, I float through my shifts at the cocktail bar. I never suggest these sleepovers that only commence at 4 am, fearing that my boyfriend will get so sick of waking up to let me in that he may throw in the towel of our relationship completely. But he suggests them, often, and he delivers me to himself in an Uber, no matter the time.

One Sunday evening, I arrive at his flat at midnight, having bolted from the quiet bar early. I shower while he settles back into bed and I consider washing my hair.

It will wet his pillows too much. He won't like that.

I soap my exhausted body, careful to avoid wetting the bun of hair balancing on top of my head. I brush my teeth, hard. My gums bleed a little. The Italian hates that I smoke.

I climb into bed next to him and reach a tentative hand over onto his side of the bed. I use it to anchor my body and I pull my limbs into his space one at a time. He is still. His hard muscles are tensed and even in the dark I know that there is irritation stirring in his wide-open eyes.

'You stink of smoke.'

'I brushed my teeth really well,' I say, my body stiffening into a rock beside his.

'Your hair stinks of smoke. You should have washed it.'

'I didn't want to wet your pillows.'

'Go shower.'

I peel back the rubbery green-yellow and I sink my teeth into the soft flesh and I get out of bed and back into the shower and I wash my hair and I say nothing when he cancels my side order of mayonnaise when we eat sushi and I want to make him happy.

I return to the bedroom, twist a white towel around wet my

hair. Twist, twist, release. Twist, twist, release. My statue love is still awake, his breath tells me. Once I am back, on my side of the bed, he opens his small mouth and poison pours out.

You need to quit that shit job.

Aren't you tired of only being a waitress?

You should be thinking about your future.

Aren't you better than being a waitress?

'You can apologise to me in the morning,' I tell him, pretending to be strong. 'I had a long shift and I'm exhausted.'

CHAPTER 27

BDSM, Erectile Dysfunction, Role-play and Anal Sex

Despite working incredibly hard, Old Lass can no longer afford the rent of the Linden house. Protector & Soul and I once again pack up our lives and find a flat nearby. Old Lass and Stinky find a cute red duplex in a neighbouring suburb. I've wrapped up my studying at the college and doodle wild, green ideas in a huge notebook while continuing to waitress.

One day The Italian tells me that Kim is looking for an editorial intern at *COSMO*, and she's expecting me to apply.

'I really need you to get this internship, Christy. It would be so good for you.'

I don't understand his words, and I wonder if he's phrased them incorrectly, but nonetheless philodendron dreams rush away from me and instead I see myself walking into an office and greeting fabulous women and writing my days away. With stiff, anxiety-laden fingers, I email Kim for the writing brief and I pour myself into the article that serves as an application. I am sitting with Old Lass at a bakery a few days later when Kim replies.

*I would be delighted if you'd like to come intern at COSMO.
We can start with a month trial, if you like, and go from there?*

When I arrive on my first day, I greet a kind woman at reception and she leads me to the *Cosmopolitan* office. Kim is seated behind a massive desk and smiles widely as she introduces me to the fashion assistant who shares the space. When I am nervous, you can either find me deathly quiet, chainsmoking in a corner, or letting my rambling words run away with me. I can't smoke in this office, obviously, what with it being 2015 and the fact that every window in the building is sealed shut. 'Anti-suicide windows,' Kim tells me. And so I chatter away about anything I can think of.

As I am shown around the office, the reality is only slightly less fabulous than what I imagined. The grey of the chairs and the beige of the floors are interrupted by bursts of colour. Everywhere I look, there are women talking and laughing. I hear tales of a first date regaled animatedly over the bubbling kettle in the kitchen. *Marie Claire* fashion interns power through the halls, all the while being swallowed whole by crisp, steamed clothes. I meet a Fashion editor and a Beauty editor and every woman who makes up the sales team, and they smile with ease and sincerity. I lose my composure entirely when Kim and I poke our heads around the corner of *Marie Claire's* Beauty office. Shelf upon shelf of perfume, nail polish, make-up and hair product perch neatly in straight lines. Kim answers my wide eyes and says, 'Wait until the beauty staff sale. People go crazy.'

That day, I publish my first ever piece of writing. When I see my name on the *Cosmopolitan* website I drink in every letter of my long surname. I message my sister, The Italian, Old Lass – my excitement spilling from me and needing somewhere to land. Indeed, these *are* 9 Reasons Why Cake is Better than Your Boyfriend. And so I spend my days talking with and learning from Kim, and as each day passes my fan-girling grows. When I arrive in the morning, the way she is sitting at her desk tells me she'd settled in there a while before. When I leave, I know her lovely bum won't be budging for some time. I quite instantly fall in love with her friendship and mentorship; the vision of her watching me salsa all those months before fading from memory with each day.

Countless toasted sandwiches devoured at my desk later, my three-month unpaid internship has come to an end. When I walk out on my last day, I cry like a child the second I am on the street, out of sight. As I wait for my Uber I consider that this must be what it feels like to want something in its entirety. The next week, I am sitting with Best eating cheese when the online editor emails me asking if I'd like to apply for a permanent position.

YES.

Wonderful. Let's get the writing test started now. Send me five article pitches. Pick one, interview an expert in the related field and write up the piece. Your deadline is in four hours.

Three and a half hours later, I hit 'send', thanks to my sexologist Elna (read: earth angel), and begin refreshing my inbox for a response.

I get the job, gallop back into the office and a few weeks in I am asked to manage all the content for a new *COSMO* microsite that focuses on sex and only sex.

And so it is not uncommon to find me at my desk, cross-legged on my swivel chair, sipping coffee out of a branded *COSMO* mug, half chatting to Kimmy and half watching porn. I see things no one should ever see, I force Kim to watch it with me, we giggle and say cunt and apologise in between our rosebud horror to the raven-haired fashion assistant who loves Jesus.

My life consists of sex. I wake up with dick on the brain, I joke, but really I do. I churn out article after article about BDSM, erectile dysfunction, role-play and anal sex. I bleed my limitlessly giving network of experts dry, and then I go to The Italian's home and explore my sexuality more devotedly than a 1000 articles would ever have allowed.

I try to speak to him about these things – about BDSM and role-play and anal sex. Some because I'm personally curious, others because I'd simply love to hear his thoughts. But one day he tells me that he doesn't like talking about sex, that he's never been with a woman who does, and it's unbecoming.

Hours later when my bum is thrashed red, streaked with

handprints, and The Italian has fallen into a deep sleep, I wonder if we can talk about the sex now. I wince as I sit down on the couch, me and my spanked booty wondering why the things that feel so natural inside a bedroom can feel so foreign outside of it.

When actual grown-ups ask me what I write about, I say fashion. Celebrity news. Snippets of actual news. Beauty products. Sometimes I say 'relationships', but never do I say sex, especially to My Father. I don't have a car, and I have barely enough money to cover my rent, let alone Uber everywhere, so again I am a child being carted around my life by my parents. And so some afternoons my unemployed father picks me up from the office in Sandton and I shove my feet firmly against the car mat and drape my jersey across my chest. I tug my short skirt as far down as it will go and I tell him that work is going well. The Italian is doing well. Everything is well. He asks me when he can meet The Italian and I know I can't put it off any longer so I invite him to my house a few days later for a pizza dinner. Protector & Soul is my soldier, armour, sanity in situations such as these. My Father arrives and greets The Italian. We eat pizza and make small talk and at the end of the lukewarm meal, my boyfriend accompanies My Father outside to the balcony for his post-meal Camel.

When I go outside to join them after washing the dishes, I find them whispering to each other. They raise their arms in the same way, flick their wrists in the same way, and tell me to go back inside and leave them be. They're discussing something privately. This is not bonding, I think as a knowing nervousness grows inside me. This is my fucking nightmare. They're in cahoots, only I don't know why, about what. But I am the only thing they have in common.

On my birthday a few weeks later, The Italian arrives at my house with a huge, nauseatingly pink box tied with a bow.

We sit on my bed as I pull at the ribbon. I lean over, my hair falling forward, and tie it around my head, a red-bow headband for the birthday girl, before lifting the lid of the box. Inside there are more bras than I have purchased in the last five years of my life combined, and enough pairs of lacy knickers that I could survive on doing my laundry only every fortnight.

In between these colours and textures is a sheet of paper folded into a paper aeroplane.

A few weeks later, we catch our flights to Cape Town, and while this is a gift to me, I know The Italian is actually trying to sell me the idea of an entire city. He wants to move there, and he wants me to go with him. He doesn't say when, and he's busy building a new business in Joburg, but each time he mentions it, he seems urgent and resolute. We check into our Airbnb, climb the impractically narrow stairs to the loft bedroom and I want to have sex but The Italian wants to unpack.

We unpack and head out to explore. We spend four days going on long drives and stopping at every third or fourth nursery or gallery-cum-pile-of-rubble-and-crafts along the way. We sing. My god, we sing. Loudly, terribly, enthusiastically, and these moments are always my favourite.

We climb Lion's Head and I argue – and lose – with my fear of heights on the way down. My eyeballs sweat as they retreat into my skull and lunge forward out of their sockets.

We have sex on the huge bed each night, and on the couch one afternoon and I think that if this is what Cape Town feels like, I might finally have been sold. I fry us gnocchi while The Italian works at night, and cook us eggs while he works in the morning. I think that there is enough time in between this to have a dream job, that these things will make for a dream life and as I write this I feel ill. And I crave fried gnocchi.

Some things, the best things, never leave you.

We return to Joburg and life continues peacefully for the next two months. I write about sex and I eat toasted sandwiches. I have my weekly dinners with Best and Mimika and my almost-daily coffees with Old Lass. The Italian, however, has had an internal shift that presents itself to me discreetly one night through his rolling eyes. As we sit on his black couch, discussing nothing and everything, I say something silly. Where two months before he would have smiled and called me a dork, he rolls his eyes and turns his face away from mine, and I shit you not when I say that in this exact moment I know he has begun falling out of love with me.

I throttle the voice in my cells so violently that for entire days at a time I am able to pretend that everything is okay. However, on the days it comes up for air, it voices its concern to Kim.

'Kimmy, The Italian and I haven't had sex in a week and a half.'

'Girl, that's so, so normal. You shouldn't overthink it.'

'But it's not normal for us,' I say, when what I want to actually say is DEAR GOD THE WORLD IS ENDING I FEEL IT IN MY BONES PLEASE GOD MAKE HIM LOVE ME AGAIN.

'Just give it a few days. He's probably just got a lot going on.'

'You're right. Thanks, Kimmy.' When what I actually want to say is BE A DOLL AND TELL ME RIGHT NOW IF ANY OF THE BOYS HAVE HEARD ANYTHING HE'S CHEATING ON ME ISN'T HE I BET SHE'S A GODDAMN ROCK CLIMBER.

Throttle, throttle, throttle. Above-par toasted sandwiches and delicious denial.

Before any of us know it, we're packing our lives into bags and heading off in different directions for our December holiday. Best and I rejoice in the knowledge that after many years of friendship, we'll finally celebrate a new-year countdown together, so we go shopping and spend money we don't have on outfits that will be wasted on the Drakensberg festival we're headed to.

I've been begging The Italian to come with us for weeks. One day he is tempted by the idea, the next he is drowning in work. Real or imagined, I can't say. Finally, the day before we leave, he tells me that he and his best friend, Boob, have decided to go to the festival too.

'We'll drive down the day after you and share a tent,' he tells me casually one day as we walk through the parking lot of the Zoo Lake public pool.

'You'll share a tent … with Boob?'

'Yip.'

'What's going on?'

WHAT THE ACTUAL FUCK, YOU SILLY LITTLE MAN. WHY WOULD YOU WANT TO SHARE A TENT WITH YOUR FRIEND WHEN YOU COULD SHARE A TENT WITH ME?

YOU'LL REGRET THIS WHEN WE DON'T HAVE A SPACE OF OUR OWN IN WHICH TO FUCK.

'You are being so weird, Italian. You have been for weeks. When you figure out what the hell is going on with you, best you let me know.'

He doesn't let me know, and by the time he arrives at the festival I am two parts tequila and one part forgetful elation. The tequila wears off though. It makes way for a hangover and the realisation that I have spent, quite literally, about four minutes in my boyfriend's company since he arrived.

'Boob and I didn't come here to drink and get fucked up. We want to go hiking and climb rocks,' he tells me when I ask him if we can spend time together.

'But it's a festival.'

OH, FUCK OFF ALREADY.

In this super healthy way, me, my mind and my boyfriend bash heads for the first two days of the festival, until the second night where I say the thing I should have said long ago.

'If you don't want to be with me, you can just end it. Really. There's no point in doing this if you're not happy.'

He says nothing.

JESUS-FUCKING-CHRIST, MEN BARELY EVER SAY ANYTHING.

I calm my mind enough to be the me, the self, I want to be in this moment.

'You make me happy, but if I don't make you happy any more, you need to say so.'

And then he speaks.

'You don't make me *unhappy*.'

OH MY GOD, HE DOES LOVE ME I'M JUST BEING CRAZY – TAKE THAT, FUCKIN' CELLS HAR-HAR-HAR – I'M SO SILLY.

Later in the night, after much vodka has been drunk and many hiking paths forgotten, we dance wildly on the grass and we kiss deeply after the countdown and as we walk to the tent that tonight we'll be sharing, I consider the notion that the way you spend new year's eve is the way you'll spend the next year of your life.

The Italian is inside of me, on top of me. The thin mattress barely lessens the blow of the hard ground beneath me. I see in my love's eyes how violent he is in this moment. His palm hovers above my face. For the last few months, it has been hovering over my face whenever he's been inside of me, on top of me.

'Hurt me,' I shout in a whisper.

And he crashes his palm, the shell of an Italian fist, down and it collides with my right cheek. My head is thrown sideways and I smile, and he finishes.

Through the netting of the tent I see Chinese lanterns floating into the black sky, and I wonder if we can talk about sex now.

Like a can of worms or Pandora's box, so something has spilled. It is dirty and wriggly like a can of worms and forbidden and mesmerising like the contents of Pandora's box.

We have never had vanilla sex, The Italian and I, but now the sprinkles we sometimes glittered on our sex have turned to salted caramel to chocolate laced with chilli to sea urchins. If I was spanked before the night in the tent, my ass is clobbered now. If my throat was squeezed gently before, it's collapsing now. If I was slapped in the tent, I am smacked now.

I come to, to see stars; I say, 'Hurt me more.'

One night, after the sex and alone on the black couch, the stars dancing around the air in the room make me realise that I have been a reckless fool.

'Italian,' I say as he walks down the hall sipping a glass of water, 'we should really have a safe word.'

He says nothing. He turns a corner into his bedroom, sits at his desk and continues working.

I think:

Tulip.

Philadelphia.

Slap, slap.

CHAPTER 28

The Italian, My Father and Sherlock-Fucking-Holmes

One night, I'm reading on The Italian's bed and he is in the shower when his phone's screen lights up on the duvet next to me.

It's a reminder. It says, 'Call Chili.'

Me and my sister and My Father are the only Chilis I know, and we're certainly the only Chilis The Italian knows. Protector & Soul wouldn't warrant a reminder of a phone call, so that leaves only one Chili.

I am Sherlock-Fucking-Holmes and I do what I should never have done, but I'm glad I did. I go into his WhatsApp and type My Father's name into the search bar.

'Hi. I want to know if you'd still be interested in helping me get Christy a car? We would finance it through your name and I'd send you the money each month.'

My sneaky boyfriend, my sneaky, blacklisted parent.

My aching heart.

'She can obviously never know.'

The Italian hasn't replied to this, the first message.

He hasn't replied to the message that came after.

But he has replied to the one about meeting for coffee to discuss my life without me ever knowing.

Yes.

When he's out the shower and back in the bedroom, I ask him if he's been speaking to My Father.

'No.'

'Well, I saw a reminder come up on your phone and it seems like it's to do with him?'

'It's not.'

'So you don't speak?'

'No.'

'Okay, because it wouldn't be the first time My Father spoke to the people closest to me behind my back. He's done it before and he shouldn't be trusted and if he gets hold of you, you should tell me.'

'Okay.'

The next day, I am back at home drinking coffee and working on my balcony. My phone rings and it's My Father. He asks if he can come over for coffee. I say yes. Mine bitter with some milk. His sickly sweet and black.

'I've fucked up, Lolo,' he says.

In his mind I am still a child, so it is easy to play dumb.

'What did you do?'

'The first night I met The Italian at your house we discussed getting you a car together because, you know, I can't get finance. I met with him this morning to discuss it and he said he's no longer comfortable doing it. I asked him not to tell you about any of this, but he said he's not willing to lie to you.'

I wonder, does truth that arrives late excuse a lie that arrived at all?

'Tell me this, what was your grand plan if The Italian and I broke up? I'd be driving around in a car I think is mine but actually belongs to my ex-boyfriend?'

'I'm so sorry,' he says. And I believe that he is, but I don't care. I consider every time over the last few months My Father has said to me, 'Lolo, women are like birds. It's a man's job to build his woman a cage. A golden cage. But he must leave the door open so she can fly free, but she must also always return to, you know … the golden cage.'

I picture myself rolling through the streets of Johannesburg, a golden cage on wheels. I finish my coffee, tell My Father I have to get back to work, and spend the day waiting for an apology from The Italian that never arrives.

When he picks me up that evening for dinner, he asks me what's wrong. 'I know about the car thing.' He assumes all my sadness and anger rest solely on the actions of My Father, and when he doesn't apologise for having lied to me, I realise there is genuinely no part of him that believes he's done anything wrong.

I eat my dinner, and for the first time in a long time I have run out of words. I don't know how to present my pain plainly, and I don't know if I want to have to any more.

Back at our desks, Kim and I discuss our sex, our hearts, our coleslaw or pasta that we made for dinner the night before.

'How's it been going? Are you having sex more regularly now?' she asks me one day.

'Yip, we are.'

I hold the truth of the kind of sex I'm having gently in my cupped palms. It scratches at my flesh and I try to give it enough room to breathe. I need to keep it alive and examine it.

It's rough, and I love it.

It's reckless. Not in a sexy way.

It is in one moment the most intimate thing I have ever experienced with another person, and in the next I feel deathly alone.

With every centimetre that keeps us apart, our emotional connection begins retreating, and our sex is used to bridge the gaps. Rather than bearing witness from within to a relationship in which the love is surely dying (from The Italian's end, at least) I revel in the newness and secrecy of how our relationship has evolved. It is fabulously distracting, but none of this occurs to me on the mornings that I streak and level layers of BB cream onto the deep purple of my face.

It won't do.

I buy base.

It works.

Then one morning I wake up in my own home, I make coffee, I smoke cigarettes, I go to the bathroom to brush my teeth. I look in the mirror. Scabs litter my face. They arch with the top of my eyebrows where the soft flesh of my forehead has burnt. They dot my top lip. I dwell, for only a moment, on memories of the bruised lip that accompanied my childhood before surveying the damage done to the sides of my face. Red and raw in some places, drying up in others, burnt welts courtesy of my attempt to rid myself of unwanted facial hair the night before. I grab the tube of hair-removal cream from the windowsill and read the 'warnings' through my chubby tears. I *did* do the patch test. I have been using this cream for years. I *did* leave it on for just the right amount of time. I *did* rinse it off rigorously.

I call Old Lass, chubby tears having given birth to sobs. When she arrives four minutes later, she is my treasure and my pharmacy. She shouts at me for having used the cream in the first place. 'Your facial hair is barely even noticeable!' she shouts and I wail in return, 'Oh puh-lease, Mom!'

She tells me to get dressed and come to the pharmacy with her so we can get the advice of someone who knows what the fuck to do, but I refuse. I feel too hideous to leave my house, and far too foolish to explain to anyone how this has happened. Old Lass leaves and I message Kim. I consider lying to her, but I know that my face won't heal for a few days at the very least. 'Kims, I've done something so stupid and I can't come into work today.'

I tell her the entire, ridiculous story, send her some photos and make her promise she won't tell anyone.

'What will you tell The Italian?'

'I'll tell him I used a face mask that was too rough on my skin.'

And so that night, at his house, I do.

'Does it hurt?' he asks.

I feel my skin pull, tighten, I feel the scabs crack around my mouth when I reply, 'Ja.'

Despite the layers of make-up, the warzone is clearly visible, each scab resembling a mountain with its peaks covered in dirty, beige snow.

That night The Italian and I climb into his bed, and we begin having sex. He is on top of me and I can see his twitching palm hovering in the air above me. I turn my face to the side, crumple my chin into my neck; I do whatever I can to make my face off limits, but I rationalise that I don't need to spell this out for him.

His open palm collides with my cheek.

I say nothing.

Tulip.

Philadelphia.

Slap, slap.

The night before the day on which The Italian and I break up, I know it's coming. I am lying on Mimika's couch, tipsy after hours spent drinking wine and eating cheese. She and Best are sound asleep in her bedroom and I type a letter to The Italian onto my phone that I know he'll never read.

I've been here before. I know what's coming. I wish so much that you still loved me.

When I return to my house the next morning, I pull on a floor-length skirt. It is red and orange and yellow, and it sits perfectly on my waist. I pull a buff (the kind they have on *Survivor*) over my head, fold it over itself and wear it as a boob tube. My scabs have healed (only to reveal glowing, fresh skin beneath – all hail the accidental chemical peel) and my skin is smooth. I make a frappe and wait for The Italian to arrive. When he does, the marrow in my bones is traumatised.

He barely says a word, so I chain-smoke and ramble.

'When did it happen?'

'When did what happen?'

'What was the moment you fell out of love with me?'

He says nothing, and I can see in his crumpled face that he feels defeated, and sore.

I tell him I want him to be happy, and if he's not then we should end it.

My nostrils swell with the scent of festival memories. Spiralling potatoes fried on a stick, spilled, sticky Jägermeister and dirty knees, and I realise that the last few months, every day since the last conversation we had about the exact same thing, has been spent trying to salvage something that had already run out of breath.

'I think we should break up,' I tell him. My heart cracks and is held by a thread of hope. I wait for him to fight me on this, to tell me I'm wrong, but he doesn't. The thread snaps. I kiss him on the cheek and watch from my balcony as he climbs into his blue car and drives away.

The succulents lining the wall whisper their suspicions of my insanity. I pour myself a glass of wine, call the girls, my fierce council, and only when they arrive do I break down. The succulents sigh in relief.

When I arrive at work on Monday, my puffy eyes implore the women in the office to lie to me.

The sales team hugs me and a loony, charismatic blonde assures me he'll be back.

'I give it a week. Men get scared. They run away, but they come back. I give him a week.'

I replace the carbohydrates that are my soul's nourishment with these words and I drink them in greedily. I spend every day of the first few weeks sitting vacantly at my desk, staring out the window into the parking lot below. I am waiting to see the top of The Italian's head, his shoes, his blue chinos, his hands carrying a bunch of flowers to me. I fear I may actually be going insane, because when I dwell on this fantasy for long enough, my heart's load actually manages to temporarily lighten. And this is how I get through my days. I wake up, drink coffee, smoke cigarettes, get dressed, arrive at work and pretend to be okay. I sit at my desk and look out the window and my mind's mirage consoles me into doing my job. I get home, immediately climb into bed, binge on Kim's *Sex & The City* box set, pass out at 6 pm and do it all over again the next day, and the day after that.

One afternoon a few weeks after the break-up, Protector & Soul finds me sitting on my bedroom floor staring into the mess that is my cupboard.

'Sissie,' I say, 'I need you to keep an eye on my eating. Don't make a big deal of it, and don't try force me to do anything. Just help me keep an eye on this.'

And so, for the weeks that follow, I walk into my bedroom to find a sandwich or toast layered with jam and cheese sitting on my bedside table, and so I begin learning how to eat again.

CHAPTER 29

Milk

Samantha Jones has restored my sanity somewhat by the time I re-emerge into the world, just strong enough to engage in small talk. I am at a day festival and feel my deep joy in the simple act of existing beginning to bubble once again.

I am digging my neatly pedicured toes into the grass when a tall, pale man takes a step closer.

'Hi.'

'Hello.'

'Has anyone ever told you that you look like Pocahontas?'

I smile at him, I let him buy me a warm beer and, because I'm not ready to kiss anyone yet, I ask him for his number.

Two weeks later I am in my bathtub and I am officially cried out. Any Italian thoughts in my mind now consist of weighing up fettuccine against penne, pesto against arrabiata.

'Hi. I just wanted to thank you for my beer.'

Protector & Soul giggles as I read out my ground-breaking message, the one that took a solid hour and frayed nerves for my pruned fingers to type.

Another two weeks of sporadic messaging go by, and I am tipsily standing in line at a bar to order a whiskey when my tall glass of milk greets me.

Within minutes, we are kissing; Milk's wingman slipping from the venue he'd just paid R60 to get into.

Between smooches, I look up into his green eyes, and I consider that he may be a most fabulous man with whom to have my first-ever one-night stand, but not tonight. Tonight I revel in the innocence of once again touching tongues with a man.

Five drinks, four shots and a few hours later, I pull Mimika off the dance floor and tell Milk that I have had a lovely time, but it's time we got home. He kisses me goodbye and Mimika and I spill happily onto the pavement, hailing an Uber with our fingertips that never arrives.

'My Uber is here,' Milk says. 'I'm more than happy to drop you girls at home on the way.'

'Oh. Is Linden on the way to your place?'

'Nowhere near.'

I smile, thank him, and the three of us pile into the back seat.

In the 15 minutes it takes to reach my house, many discoveries are made in this car. The most enlightening being that Mimika is in fact only half as drunk as she thought she was. The cause of her wobbly legs not being solely based on the number of vodka sodas she's inhaled all evening, but rather the unreliable heel of her left boot, which has come loose at some point during the night. I, in the meantime, discover that I am ravenous and in desperate need of McDonald's chips. Milk discovers that he has no say in the matter; we will impede his healthy lifestyle come hell or McFlurry, and I discover that I'm not just yet done with him on this evening.

When we pull up in front of my building, I ask him if he'd like to come up for tea.

'I love tea,' he says.

'But it's just for tea,' I warn him.

'I love just tea.'

We sit at the dining table and eat the cardboard meals that in a few hours we will all desperately regret, while Mimika's big brother, Druncan sleeps like the dead on my couch, having absconded from the bar hours before us, taking my spare keys with him.

When Mimika goes off to my bed, Milk and I drink wine on the balcony and, between kisses, talk about everything. And, in the case of Milk and I, there is literally *everything* to talk about. I have nothing in common with this person, and I adore it. He is an engineer and a Sci-Fi nerd and his mind is as interesting as his biceps are delectable. He quizzes me on the scientific names of the plants that drown my balcony and I tell him that one of my hobbies over the last few weeks has included testing out my new vibrator on the balcony when no one is home.

By 5 am we are talked and kissed out and I invite him to stay over.

'Just for cuddles.'

'I love just cuddles.'

We settle on a couch adjacent to the one that still has a drunk gay man passed out on it, and Milk wraps his arms around me, buries his head in my neck and falls asleep, and I fall asleep too.

An hour later I wake up, inhale Milk's skin, which smells of holiday and incense, and I decide that *today* is indeed the day to have my first-ever one-night stand.

I roll over to find that he is also awake. We kiss, quietly. Druncan hasn't stirred once. I pull my shorts off under the covers.

'Are you sure?' Milk whispers.

'Yes. Do you have a condom?' I ask.

He nods and cradles me with one strong arm while he reaches over, pulls his wallet out of his jeans lying crumpled on the floor and retrieves a condom.

I am cheeky and sneaky and because there is no room on this couch, I pretend I am the kind of woman who has thighs built for being on top.

We have the sex, and it is gentle and delicious and the guilt I feel for shtooping someone on a couch next to my sleeping friend is smothered by the excitement and comfort I feel with Milk.

He leaves not long after, and the sleeping troops all wake and gather one by one on the balcony to share stories over coffee.

'Christy-nu! I can't believe you had sex on your couch while my brother was in the room!' Mimika says.

Just then Druncan emerges from the lounge wearing his hangover heavily.

'Yip, she did. And, girl, your boobs looked *amazing*! I mean. I didn't *watch* … but I didn't *not* watch either.'

Over the next few months, my time with Milk is spent eating sushi, exploring gentle sex, drinking wine, and talking. It is intoxicatingly simple and lovely and, without meaning to, I fall very much in love with my first-ever failed attempt at no-strings-attached, single-girl sex.

And then, four months into knowing Milk, the last thread of patience I have for My Father snaps. Protector & Soul is working at a hospital one day when she phones me in tears of frustration.

'Dad's done it again. He sent me something so inappropriate and I don't know what to do any more,' she tells me.

I tell her to forward me everything, and with each screenshot I scroll through I feel the bile rise within me.

Do you have a sense of humour?

This is always how he prefaces his indecency. My sister and I learnt years before to always say, 'No.'

But this doesn't stop him. 'Sense of humour' or not, he will send and say whatever he likes, and this time it is a picture of a naked woman brandishing a strap-on dildo.

I read through my sister's response to him. She lays her horror out plainly.

I don't understand why you insist on sending these things to us. How many times do we have to say 'no'?

Why the hell do you think it is appropriate to send your daughters this kind of stuff?

How many times do we have to tell you it makes us uncomfortable?

I read his responses.

You and your sister are hypocrites. Christy can ask me to pick up her contraception from the pharmacy but I can't make jokes with you?

I read my sister's reply.

The fact that you are comparing your daughter's health to the shit you send us shows how insane you are. They are not the same thing.

And I read one thing and the next thing and my nausea turns to rage. I message My Father, tell him that I'm tired of him, of what he puts my sister and me through. I tell him I think it's best if we don't have a relationship any more.

When Protector & Soul gets home a few hours later, we make coffee and settle into the couch for a communication meeting. I burst. Years' worth of pain spills from me, runs from my nose. I am like a child who, despite running out of tears, hasn't yet cried enough. I choke on My Father's sickness. My sister cries with me. My nostrils and my tear ducts and my secrets flood the room and we finally talk plainly about the things we've grown accustomed to dancing around.

About the trips to Hillbrow and the crack and the porn magazines lying around the house and the comatose man who wasn't watching over us when he should have been and about the disgustingly inappropriate things he used to show us when he eventually rose from the dead and the chaos and the chaos and the chaos. The leather-belt threats and the bath-time sadness.

Some things are easier than others to talk about. We watched, through a child's eyes; we've seen what drugs can do. But this never did settle within us. Like little adventurers we would gaze out of the car windows and return to the Rosebank house, climb beneath the orange covers and declare wildly and to ourselves that our lives, one day when we're big – because when you are a child your life is not your own – would never be like this. And we meant it. In this way, I suppose, instead of addiction raging within us like it did our parents, it settles around us. An armour of knowledge of what not to do. But it is heavy to carry and leaves little room within its rigidity for exploration of our own. And so I envy twentysomethings who holiday in Mykonos and take ecstasy on the beach. The twentysomethings who can drink another drink without checking themselves and interrogating their souls in the mirror of the bathroom of the bar, quietly and alone, asking themselves:

Are you still in control?

Are you still there?

In all the scenarios that could have materialised for two hairy young Greek girls raised by addict parents, I feel like this is one of the best. We're tough, with just enough room within our cracks to let some hurt in. Just enough hurt to prevent us from becoming raging assholes, but not enough hurt to make us sad people. Sad people don't become successful people. Sad people become addicts. And herein lies the daily struggle for the child of the addict. Be happy, but not too happy. Anything too happy feels insincere. Anything too happy feels out of control and dangerous.

Be sad, but not sad enough that you are weak. Be strong in confronting feelings. Not because you actually want to, but because you know they'll eat you alive if you don't. People who are eaten alive by their feelings become addicts.

Our ability to give each other the freedom to alternate between the roles of tiger and mouse has come with maturity. It's a miracle when the older sibling has grown up enough to shrink into a mouse. To feel her feelings. It's a miracle when the younger sibling is able to grow into a tiger. And so this is how we manage our time, our hearts, and our relationship. Today I will be tough so that you can fall to pieces, and tomorrow we'll switch, okay?

We have dissected within an inch of its life the reality of the child raised by addicts, but what of the women raised by men such as My Father? His is a being where all the worst parts of being a woman in our society have gathered, bred, and breathed us into life.

Two parts Greek, two parts addict, one part resilient woman, one part sick man.

And so we sit, two confused women still healing our child selves, and we turn our keen eye and scalpel to the wound we've not yet addressed, cleaned, dressed.

And so I tell my sister everything. How robbed I feel of normalcy and ownership of my sexuality and how sore and infiltrated my life is because of this man, this man who is sick and who has handed us his sickness at every turn since we were just girls and I feel a truth I thought I'd die from before saying, burning the tip of my tongue and my taste buds want this poison out.

'He stole my fucking ability to orgasm.'

I say it, and there it is. And here it is in words and I wasn't and am not finished yet.

'I have had one orgasm in my life, sissie,' I say, and I am so ashamed that I want to die.

'That's okay, Christ. Lots of women have trouble reaching orgasm.'

'No, I know, but that's not it. It's about the one orgasm I did have.'

'What do you mean?'

I want to die I am so ashamed.

I begin speaking and I am sucked back in time where I land, with a lukewarm thud, on my bed in the cottage in the blue house, where my 18-year-old thighs are welcoming Olive Oil into their fold.

I have just had a fight with Old Lass about life and men and the shit men she has brought into our lives and I curse her for having married My Father and she smiles and tells me it was worth it because I am here, in the world. I tell her that if I wasn't she wouldn't know any better anyway. 'You'd have married a nice Jewish man and would have some nice Jew-ish children instead and you wouldn't have even known to miss me.'

And so I am petulant and bored and having sex with Olive Oil on my burnt-orange duvet while considering my life, its chaos, the walking joy-hurricanes that barrel through my raspberry-tinted temperament, when My Father pops into my head.

Like a joint I once smoked by the seaside that was laced with god-knows-what.

The joint that left demons whispering to me, hallucinations enveloping me, an innocent thing turned to horror in one moment, Olive Oil's finger finds my sweet spot at the perfectly incorrect time. My ears begin to ring, my toes are violently sucked by angels, and I explode into my first orgasm.

I am yanked back to reality and I am on the couch now. My shame is scrambling for cover. It claws its way along my blue coffee table and takes refuge under my favourite ashtray; yellow. It scuttles along my parquet floor and wraps itself in the folds of the thick curtains. It dives headfirst into my iced coffee and breathes quietly from within a hollowed-out ice cube. It exists everywhere, out of sight.

I look up, expecting to see Tiger in tatters, but there instead is the inexplicably calm and unaltered face of my Protector & Soul. She takes me, her tiny Mouse, into her arms and nothing that matters most has changed; everything that needed to give way has shattered.

I breathe; look around. My yellow ashtray is still, undeterred by my imaginings and confessions. My thick curtains are no match for the breeze and, as they billow, they reveal only empty space, Christmas beetles and worst nightmares being carried into the air. My ice cubes melt and I down my coffee and there is nothing, not one thing, left at the bottom of my glass. Nothing that matters most has changed; my shame has not been granted refuge since its eviction.

I have not burst into flames.

A few nights later, Milk and I pull into his driveway. Once he has parked the car, I tell him I am ready to talk about the pain I have been carrying around in my eyes for the last few days.

'So you know I told you about all the stuff my sister and I went through as kids? That's not really all that happened.'

This delicious thing, this contagious truth …

Spill.

Spill.

Acknowledgements

To all the people who have never made me feel like I am 'too much'. My dinner people.

Nicole, my gobble gobble who let me share our story even though it was kak sore for both of us.

Alexander, for singing so beautifully and being the most special little man.

Nona, who I interrogated about our family's history during the writing of this book. Thank you for taking care of me then, with strawberry pops and sanity, and now, with coffee and love.

Nic, my deathseat cousin. Thank you for always taking me seriously and treating me like a grown-up (even when I wore too much eyeliner and was convinced that nobody understood me).

Granny Witch, for being my biggest supporter (even when I write about anal sex). If my grandmother can deal, everyone else can deal too.

Monika and Meagan (in no particular order – shut up), for piecing my peace with wine, yiros and limitless love. For coming with me to every gynae appointment, driving me to therapy, heartbreak-dancing with me. You're worth more than one trillion sparkly gems. And you're both the Beyoncé.

Kims, for being my mentor and the best, bravest friend a girl could have. Thanks for loving me even though I'm only twelve.

Azeemah, for making me believe I was brave enough to leave the end of this story alone.

Melinda freakin' Ferguson. Thank you for convincing me to pretend everyone in my life was dead while I wrote this. You are a hurricane woman, and you are so inspiring.

Daniel, my brilliant love. You make me feel immeasurably powerful. For you, anything.

And mostly, to my mama with the caramel core. Dotty, thank you for putting me first and encouraging me to write it all. Yours is the most gorgeous heart.